Taco Cookbook

An Easy Taco Cookbook with Delicious Taco Recipes

By
BookSumo Press
All rights reserved

Published by BookSumo Press:
http://www.booksumo.com

Table of Contents

How to Make a Taco 7

Taco Gratin 8

Full Bajas 9

Dorm Room Taco Tuesdays 10

How to Make Taco Shells with Cheese 11

Moroccan Taco Dump Dinner 12

Taco Pies 101 13

Mexican Flat Tacos 14

Laurel Canyon Taco Soup 15

Memphis Fish Tacos with White Sauce 16

Ketogenic Taco Casserole 17

Catalina's Lunch Box Salad 18

Authentic Mexican Cheesecake 19

How to Make Taco Sauce 20

Mexican Monday's Ground Beef 21

Picante Taco Cups 22

Tacos Enchiladas 23

Ballantyne Taco Soup 24

Tacos Gonzalez 25

East LA Refried Casserole 26

Whole Wheat Tacos 27

Sonoma Chicken Tacos 28

Barcelona Shrimp Tacos 29

After-School Pasta Tacos 30

Lorna's Bruschetta Mexicana 31

Pinwheel Taco 32

Skinny Hot Fish Tacos 33

Garden Party Tacos 34

Spicy Jalapeno Potato Tacos 35

Messy Shrimp Tacos with Cilantro Dressing 36

Mexican Lunch Box Fries 37

Alameda Tacos with Onion Flakes 38

Rust Belt Tacos 39

Katrina's Mesa Lasagna 40

Creamy Sirloin and Pasta Taco Casserole 41

Mi Linda's Tacos 42

Carolina Cornbread Taco Casserole 43

Chili Taco Ranch Wheels 44

Taco Bites 45

Mesa Cod Tacos 46

Italian Tacos with Tortilla Chips 47

State Fair Tacos 48

Wednesday's Ground Beef Skillet 49

Con Queso Taco Bake 50

Ciudad Tacos 51

Saucy Beef Taco Casserole 52

Mexican Popcorn 53

Refried Taco Pizza 54

Mushroom Tacos 55

Taco Volcanoes 56

Chipotle Pollo Guisado Tacos 57

Santiago Taco Pan 58

Manhattan Island Taco Bagels 59

Classic Mac and Cheese Taco Casserole 60

Spicy Tacos with Jalapeno Salsa and Lime Cream 61

Chipotle Taco Burgers 63

Taco Dip Morena 64

Taco Salad Madura's 65

Orange Sirloin Tacos 66

Grilled Halibut Tacos 67

Spicy Taco Meatballs with Honey Sauce 68

Acapulco Tacos 69

Nutty Tacos 70

Crunchy Burrito Style Tacos 71

Tijuana Tacos 72

Taco Tenders 73

Bell Tilapia Tacos with Peach Salsa 74

Cheddar Tacos with Lime Dressing 75

Carne Asada and Homemade Salsa 76

Ventura Tacos 77

Portuguese Breakfast Tacos 78

Cast Iron Tacos 79

Hot Crispy Taco Wings 80

California Cream Tacos 81

Mexican Cheesy Bread 82

Taco Fiesta Pan 83

Elizabeth's Taco Family Casserole 84

Mexicorn Tacos 85

Chicago Deep Dish Taco 86

Japanese Beef Sausage Tacos 87

Black Tacos with Brown Rice 88

Mexican Tacos Sea Shells 89

Hot Taco Scoops 90

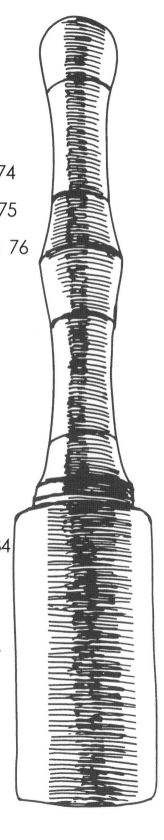

Onondaga Territory Tacos 91

Southwest Quiches 92

Saucy Taco Noodles Casserole 93

Secret Tacos 94

Spanish Style Taco Pan 95

Halibut BBQ Tacos 96

Gyros Style Tacos with Yogurt Sauce 97

Seasoned Taco Chips 98

Creamy Taco Stroganoff Casserole 99

Latin Garlic Steak Tacos 100

How to Make a Taco

🥣 Prep Time: 10 mins
🕐 Total Time: 20 mins

Servings per Recipe: 1
Calories 162.5
Fat 11.3g
Cholesterol 51.4mg
Sodium 49.9mg
Carbohydrates 0.0g
Protein 14.0g

Ingredients
1 lb ground beef
1 packet taco seasoning mix
tomatoes, chopped
lettuce, shredded
onion, chopped
black olives, sliced
shredded cheese
sour cream
taco sauce or picante sauce
corn chips

Directions
1. Place a large pan over medium heat. Cook in it the beef for 8 min. discard the grease.
2. Mix in the taco seasoning. Cook them for 2 extra min.
3. Spoon the beef mixture into the taco shells followed by some tomato, onion, olives, cheese, sour cream, taco sauce and corn chips.
4. Enjoy.

TACO
Gratin

Prep Time: 15 mins
Total Time: 1 hr 25 mins

Servings per Recipe: 4
Calories   732.3
Fat   40.0g
Cholesterol   142.8mg
Sodium   1892.5mg
Carbohydrates   57.2g
Protein   43.7g

Ingredients

- 1 lb ground beef
- 1 packages au gratin potatoes
- 1 cans whole kernel corn, undrained
- 1 cans stewed tomatoes, undrained
- 3/4 C. milk
- 1/2 C. water
- 2 tbsp taco seasoning
- 2 C. shredded cheddar cheese

Directions

1. Before you do anything, preheat the oven to 350 F. Grease a casserole dish.
2. Place a large pan over medium heat. Brown in it the beef for 9 min. discard the grease.
3. Mix in the potato with corn, tomatoes, milk, water and taco seasoning. Spoon the mixture into the casserole.
4. Cover the casserole with a piece of foil. Place it in the oven and cook it for 1 h 5 min to 1 h 10 min.
5. Discard the foil and top the gratin with shredded cheese. Bake it for an extra 6 min.
6. Serve your taco gratin warm with your favorite toppings.
7. Enjoy.

Full Bajas

Prep Time: 8 hrs
Total Time: 8 hrs 25 mins

Servings per Recipe: 8
Calories   701.3
Fat   31.2g
Cholesterol   115.6mg
Sodium   1451.7mg
Carbohydrates   61.9g
Protein   45.8g

Ingredients
- 3 lbs flank steaks
- 1/3 C. white vinegar
- 1/2 C. soy sauce
- 4 garlic cloves, minced
- 2 limes, juice of
- 1/2 C. olive oil
- 1 tsp salt
- 1 tsp ground black pepper
- 1 tsp white pepper
- 1 tsp garlic powder
- 1 tsp chili powder
- 1 tsp dried oregano
- 1 tsp ground cumin
- 1 tsp paprika
- 1 white onion, chopped
- 1/2 C. chopped fresh cilantro
- 1 lime, juice of
- 2 large tomatoes, chopped
- 2 jalapeno peppers, chopped
- 1 white onion, quartered
- 4 garlic cloves, peeled
- 4 dried red chile pods
- 1 pinch salt and pepper, to taste
- 1 (32 oz.) packages corn tortillas
- 2 C. grated Cotija cheese
- 2 limes, cut into wedges

Directions
1. Before you do anything, preheat the oven to 450 F.
2. Get a mixing bowl: Mix in the vinegar, soy sauce, 4 cloves of garlic, juice of two limes and olive oil.
3. Add the salt, black pepper, white pepper, garlic powder, chili powder, oregano, cumin and paprika to make the marinade.
4. Get a roasting dish: Place in it the steak then pour the marinade all over it. Cover it with a plastic wrap and place it in the fridge for 2 to 8 h.
5. To make the onion relish:
6. Get small mixing bowl: Stir in it 1 chopped white onion, cilantro and the juice of 1 lime.
7. To make the salsa:
8. Place a large pan over medium heat: Cook in it the chile pods for 2 min. Place them in a bowl of water and let them sit for 35 min.
9. Get another roasting dish: Place in it the tomatoes, 1 onion, jalapenos and 4 cloves of garlic. Bake them for 22 min.
10. Get food processor: Place in it the baked veggies and blend them smooth.
11. Place a large pan over medium heat: Heat in it the vegetable oil.
12. Drain the steak and slice it into strips. Cook them in the hot oil for 6 to 8 min until they are done.
13. Heat the tortillas then top them with the steak slices, onion relish and hot salsa. Garnish them with some cheese then serve them.
14. Enjoy.

DORM ROOM
Taco Tuesdays

Prep Time: 15 mins
Total Time: 8 hr 25 mins

Servings per Recipe: 6
Calories 228.3
Fat 6.9g
Cholesterol 74.8mg
Sodium 1187.2mg
Carbohydrates 17.9g
Protein 24.8g

Ingredients
1 1/2 lbs boneless beef chuck roast
1 medium onion, sliced
1 C. water
1 packages taco seasoning mix
1 jars taco sauce
1 cans diced green chilies
1 package taco shells
shredded lettuce
chopped tomato
shredded cheddar cheese
sour cream

Directions
1. Get a mixing bowl: Whisk in it the seasoning mix with water.
2. Stir the beef with onion, a pinch of salt and pepper in a slow cooker.
3. Pour the water mix all over them. Put on the lid and cook them for 7 h on low.
4. Once the time is up, drain the beef and shred it. Add to it the chilies with taco sauce. Toss them to coat to make the filling.
5. Place a large pan over medium heat. Heat in it the tortillas.
6. Place the tortillas on serving plates. Place the beef mixture over them then fold them.
7. Serve your tacos right away with your favorite toppings.
8. Enjoy.

How to Make Taco Shells with Cheese

Prep Time: 2 mins
Total Time: 3 mins

Servings per Recipe: 1
Calories	151.6
Fat	12.4g
Cholesterol	39.5mg
Sodium	233.6mg
Carbohydrates	0.4g
Protein	9.3g

Ingredients
1/3 C. cheddar cheese
parchment paper

Directions
1. Line up a small baking sheet with a parchment paper. Spread in it 1/3 C. of cheese in a thin layer.
2. Place in the microwave and cook it for 1 min on high.
3. Bend the parchment paper with cheese slightly in the shape of a taco shell while the cheese is soft.
4. Place it aside and let it cool down completely.
5. Fill it with some taco seasoned meat, lettuce, tomatoes, cheese, and sour cream.
6. Enjoy.

MOROCCAN Taco Dump Dinner

Prep Time: 10 mins
Total Time: 8 hr 10 mins

Servings per Recipe: 12
Calories   74.5
Fat   0.7g
Cholesterol   0.0mg
Sodium   143.5mg
Carbohydrates   12.8g
Protein   4.7g

Ingredients
1 C. chopped onion
1 garlic clove, minced
1 tsp canola oil
1 C. dry lentils, rinsed
1 tbsp chili powder
2 tsp ground cumin
1 tsp oregano
14 oz. water
2 vegetable bouillon cubes
1 C. salsa

Directions
1. Stir all the ingredients in a greased crockpot. Put on the lid and cook them for 10 on low while stirring them often.
2. Add water to the mixture if needed. Spoon the mixture into taco shells then serve them with your favorite toppings.
3. Enjoy.

Taco Pies 101

Prep Time: 30 mins
Total Time: 55 mins

Servings per Recipe: 4
Calories   711.8
Fat   28.2g
Cholesterol   160.1mg
Sodium   1885.1mg
Carbohydrates   71.8g
Protein   42.4g

Ingredients
- 1 lb lean ground beef
- 1 packages taco seasoning mix
- 1 C. shredded cheddar cheese
- 2 tbsp water
- 2 packages refrigerated crescent dinner rolls
- 1 medium bell pepper
- 1 C. salsa
- 3 C. lettuce, shredded
- 1 medium tomatoes
- 1/4 C. onion, chopped
- 1/2 C. pitted ripe black olives
- sour cream

Directions
1. Before you do anything, preheat the oven to 375. Line up a baking sheet with some parchment paper.
2. Place a large pan over medium heat. Cook in it the beef for 8 min. Turn off the heat and discard the fat.
3. Get a large mixing bowl: Toss in it the beef with taco seasoning, water and cheese.
4. Place the crescent dough on working surface and unroll them.
5. Arrange them on the lined up pan in a circle with the pointy end facing outside of the circle.
6. Place the beef filling in the middle of each triangle then pull the pointy end to the middle to cover the filling.
7. Press them slightly to seal them. Place the pan in the oven and cook them for 22 to 26 min.
8. Get a mixing bowl: Toss in it the lettuce and chop tomato, onion, olives, and bell pepper. Place the mixture in the middle.
9. Serve your taco plate warm right away with your favorite toppings.
10. Enjoy.

MEXICAN
Flat Tacos

Prep Time: 20 mins
Total Time: 25 mins

Servings per Recipe: 4
Calories   365.0
Fat   23.8g
Cholesterol   63.8mg
Sodium   783.7mg
Carbohydrates   18.2g
Protein   19.3g

Ingredients

1/4 C. mayonnaise
2 tsp minced jalapenos, slices
2 tsp jalapeno juice, from jar
3/4 tsp sugar
1/2 tsp cumin
1/2 tsp paprika
1/8 tsp cayenne pepper
1/8 tsp garlic powder
1 dash salt

4 flour tortillas
4 chicken tenderloins
1 C. shredded cheddar cheese
1 C. shredded Monterey jack cheese
2 slices process American cheese

Directions

1. Get a mixing bowl: Whisk in it all the sauce ingredients. Place it aside.
2. Place a large griddle pan over medium heat. Heat some vegetable oil in it.
3. Season the tenderloins with some salt and pepper. Cook them in the hot griddle for 4 to 6 min on each side or until they are done.
4. Drain the tenderloins aside and thinly slice them. Place them aside.
5. Place a large pan over medium heat. Place in it a tortilla, top it with 1/4 C. of each shredded cheese and 1/2 cheese slice on one side of it.
6. Place 1/4 C. of the sliced chicken over the cheese. Pour 1 tbsp of the sauce mix over the empty side of the tortilla.
7. Pull the empty side over the side with the filling. Push it down slightly and let it side for a minute or two until the cheese melts.
8. Repeat the process with the remaining ingredients to make 3 more tacos.
9. Serve your tacos right away with your favorite toppings.
10. Enjoy.

Laurel Canyon Taco Soup

Prep Time: 10 mins
Total Time: 2 hrs 10 mins

Servings per Recipe: 8
Calories   339.2
Fat   9.9g
Cholesterol   42.5mg
Sodium   729.6mg
Carbohydrates   43.4g
Protein   22.3g

Ingredients
1 cans pinto beans
1 cans white beans
1 cans corn
1 cans Rotel tomatoes & chilies
1 cans diced tomatoes
1 cans diced green chilies
1 envelopes taco seasoning mix
1 ranch dressing mix
1 lb shredded chicken

Directions
1. Get a mixing bowl: Place a large pan over medium heat. Heat in it a splash of oil. Cook in it the meat for 8 min.
2. Drain the meat and transfer it to a slow cooker. Stir in the rest of the ingredients with a pinch of salt and pepper.
3. Put on the lid and cook the soup for 4 h on low or 2 h on high.
4. Serve your taco soup hot right away with your favorite toppings.
5. Enjoy.

MEMPHIS
Fish Tacos with White Sauce

Prep Time: 15 mins
Total Time: 30 mins

Servings per Recipe: 6
Calories   258.9
Fat   14.1g
Cholesterol   42.4mg
Sodium   155.2mg
Carbohydrates   16.8g
Protein   15.6g

Ingredients
1/2 C. sour cream
1/2 C. mayonnaise
1/4 C. chopped fresh cilantro
1 package taco seasoning mix, divided
1 lb cod
2 tbsp vegetable oil
2 tbsp lemon juice
1 packages taco shells, warmed
shredded cabbage

chopped tomato
lime juice
taco sauce

Directions
1. Get a small mixing bowl: Whisk in it the sour cream, mayonnaise, cilantro and 2 tbsp seasoning mix to make the dressing.
2. Get a large mixing bowl: Toss in it the fish, vegetable oil, lemon juice and rest of the seasoning mix.
3. Place a large pan over medium heat. Stir in it the dish mix then cook them for 6 min while stirring often.
4. Spoon the mix while it is warm to the taco shells. Drizzle over it the white dressing.
5. Serve your tacos right away with your favorite toppings.
6. Enjoy.

Ketogenic Taco Casserole

Prep Time: 25 mins
Total Time: 1 hrs 15 mins

Servings per Recipe: 8
Calories   468.6
Fat   37.6g
Cholesterol   197.1mg
Sodium   538.4mg
Carbohydrates   3.7g
Protein   28.4g

Ingredients

- 4 oz. cream cheese, softened
- 3 eggs
- 1/3 C. heavy cream
- 1/2 tsp taco seasoning mix
- 8 oz. cheddar cheese, shredded
- 1 lb ground beef
- 3 tsp taco seasoning mix
- 1/4 C. tomato sauce
- 4 oz. chopped green chilies
- 8 oz. cheddar cheese, shredded

Directions

1. Before you do anything, preheat the oven to 375 F. Grease a casserole dish with a cooking spray.
2. Get a mixing bowl: Mix in it the eggs with cream cheese until they become creamy. Mix in the heavy cream with taco seasoning.
3. Lay the cheese in the bottom of the casserole. Pour the cream mixture over the cheese layer.
4. Cook it in the oven for 27 to 32 min. Let sit for 7 min.
5. Place a large pan over medium heat. Cook in it the beef for 10 min. discard the fat.
6. Mix in it the taco seasoning, with chilies, tomato sauce, a pinch of salt and pepper. Sprinkle the cheese on top.
7. Lower the oven heat to 350 F. Place in it the taco casserole and cook it for 22 min.
8. Serve your taco casserole warm with your favorite toppings.
9. Enjoy.

CATALINA'S
Lunch Box Salad

Prep Time: 30 mins
Total Time: 30 mins

Servings per Recipe: 20
Calories 237.5
Fat 17.5g
Cholesterol 41.3mg
Sodium 291.1mg
Carbohydrates 7.9g
Protein 13.2g

Ingredients

- 2 lbs lean ground beef
- 2 packages taco seasoning mix
- 2 C. grated cheddar cheese
- 1 red onion, chopped
- 1 yellow onion, chopped
- 2 heads iceberg lettuce, chopped
- 4 tomatoes, chopped
- 2 avocados, peeled and chopped
- 1 1/2 C. black olives, sliced
- 12 C. nacho chips (Doritos), crushed
- 1 bottles Catalina dressing

Directions

1. Place a large pan over medium heat. Cook in it the onion with beef for 12 min.
2. Stir in the 1 package taco seasoning mix. Turn off the heat and let it sit for few minutes to cool down.
3. Get a large mixing bowl: Toss in it the lettuce, tomatoes, cheddar cheese, avocados, red onion, olives, and the second package of taco seasoning mix.
4. Stir in the cooked beef and onion mix. Season them with some salt and pepper.
5. Drizzle the dressing over the salad followed by the crushed Doritos. Serve your salad right away with your favorite toppings.
6. Enjoy.

Authentic Mexican Cheesecake

Prep Time: 24 hrs
Total Time: 24 hrs 35 mins

Servings per Recipe: 18
Calories 211.3
Fat 19.8g
Cholesterol 77.8mg
Sodium 263.6mg
Carbohydrates 4.1g
Protein 5.2g

Ingredients

- 3 tsp cornmeal
- 3 (8 oz.) packages cream cheese, softened
- 1 envelope taco seasoning
- 1/2 C. sour cream
- 1/2 C. salsa
- 2 eggs, beaten
- 1 C. shredded Monterey jack pepper cheese
- 1 cans chopped green chilies, drained
- 1/2 C. chopped black olives
- 1 C. sour cream
- 1/4 C. sliced black olives
- 1/4 C. sliced green onion
- 1/4 C. sliced cherry tomatoes
- 1 jalapeno pepper, sliced

Directions

1. Before you do anything, preheat the oven to 350 F. Grease a springform dish with a cooking spray.
2. Spread in it the cornmeal in an even layer. Place it aside.
3. Get a large mixing bowl: Cream in it the cream cheese. Mix in the taco seasoning, sour cream and salsa.
4. Mix in the eggs, pepper jack cheese and chilies. Stir the olives into the mixture with a pinch of salt and pepper.
5. Spread it over the oatmeal layer. Place the pan in the oven and let it cook for 32 to 36 min.
6. Place the cake pan aside to cool down for 60 min.
7. Coat the whole taco cheesecake with sour cream. Top it with the olives, onions, tomatoes and jalapeno slices.
8. Serve your taco cheesecake with your favorite toppings.
9. Enjoy.

HOW TO MAKE
Taco Sauce

Prep Time: 5 mins
Total Time: 25 mins

Servings per Recipe: 4
Calories 23.8
Fat 0.3g
Cholesterol 0.0mg
Sodium 304.9mg
Carbohydrates 4.8g
Protein 1.1g

Ingredients

1 (8 oz.) cans tomato sauce
1/3 C. water
1/4 tsp chili powder
1 1/2 tsp cumin
1 1/2 tsp instant minced onion
1 tbsp white vinegar
1/2 tsp garlic powder
1/2 tsp garlic salt
1/4 tsp paprika
1/4 tsp sugar
1/4 tsp cayenne pepper

Directions

1. Place a small saucepan over medium heat. Stir in it all the ingredients.
2. Bring it to a simmer. Let it cook for 16 to 22 min. Turn off the heat and let it cool down completely.
3. Serve your sauce right away or place it in the fridge until ready you're to serve it.
4. Enjoy.

Mexican Monday's Ground Beef

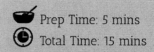 Prep Time: 5 mins
Total Time: 15 mins

Servings per Recipe: 4
Calories 279.9
Fat 17.4g
Cholesterol 77.1mg
Sodium 690.5mg
Carbohydrates 7.3g
Protein 22.2g

Ingredients
- 1 lb ground beef
- 1/4 C. flour
- 1 tbsp chili powder
- 1 tsp salt
- 1/2 tsp minced onion
- 1/2 tsp paprika
- 1/4 tsp onion powder
- 1/8 tsp garlic powder
- 1/8 tsp cumin
- 1/2 C. water

Directions
1. Get a mixing bowl: Mix in it the beef, flour, chili powder, onion, paprika, onion powder, garlic powder, cumin and salt.
2. Place a large pan over medium heat. Heat in it the water. Add the beef mixture and cook them for 10 to 12 min while stirring it often.
3. Serve your taco meat warm.
4. Enjoy.

PICANTE
Taco Cups

Prep Time: 5 mins
Total Time: 15 mins

Servings per Recipe: 1
Calories   79.7
Fat   3.4g
Cholesterol   16.4mg
Sodium   267.2mg
Carbohydrates   6.3g
Protein   5.7g

Ingredients
24 wonton wrappers
1 lb hamburger
1 packages taco seasoning mix
1/2 C. salsa or 1/2 C. picante sauce
3 tbsp salsa
1 C. shredded cheese
sour cream
olive
guacamole

Directions
1. Before you do anything, preheat the oven to 425.
2. Place a large pan over medium heat. Cook in it the hamburger for 8 min. discard the fat.
3. Mix in it the taco seasoning with 1/2 C. of salsa or picante sauce. Cook them for 4 to 6 min.
4. Grease some muffin pans. Place a wonton wrapper in each muffin C. Divide the beef mixture between them followed by the remaining sauce and cheese.
5. Place the pans in the oven and cook them for 8 to 9 min until they become golden brown.
6. Top your taco C. with some salsa, sour cream, olives and guacamole.
7. Enjoy.

Tacos Enchiladas

🥣 Prep Time: 20 mins
⏱ Total Time: 40 mins

Servings per Recipe: 4
Calories   1037.2
Fat   49.5g
Cholesterol   131.9mg
Sodium   3477.7mg
Carbohydrates   94.3g
Protein   51.5g

Ingredients
- 1 lb ground beef
- 1 cans refried beans
- 1 cans cream of mushroom soup
- 2 cans green enchilada sauce
- 1 package flour tortilla
- 1 C. shredded Monterey jack cheese
- 1 C. shredded cheddar cheese
- diced onion
- diced tomato
- shredded lettuce
- extra shredded Monterey jack cheese
- shredded cheddar cheese
- sour cream
- guacamole

Directions
1. Before you do anything, preheat the oven to 375. Grease a casserole dish with a cooking spray.
2. Place a large pan over medium heat. Cook in the beef for 8 min. discard the fat.
3. Mix in the refried beans. Turn off the heat and let it sit for few minutes.
4. Place the tortillas in the microwave for 20 sec to soften.
5. Place a tortilla on a working surface. Spread in it 2 tbsp of the beef mixture followed by 1 tsp of onion.
6. Roll the tortilla over the filling and place it in the greased casserole. Repeat the process with the remaining tortillas and filling.
7. Get a large mixing bowl: Stir in it mushroom soup and green chile enchilada sauce. Drizzle the mixture all over the tortillas.
8. Sprinkle the cheese on top. Place the casserole in the oven and let it cook for 22 min. Let it rest for 6 min.
9. Serve your taco casserole with your favorite toppings.
10. Enjoy.

BALLANTYNE
Taco Soup

Prep Time: 15 mins
Total Time: 1 hr

Servings per Recipe: 8
Calories   337.9
Fat   2.2g
Cholesterol   0.0mg
Sodium   1053.1mg
Carbohydrates   66.1g
Protein   18.8g

Ingredients
1 cans black beans
1 cans pinto beans
1 cans navy beans
1 cans black-eyed peas
1 cans green beans
1 cans corn
1 small onion, chopped
1 cans tomato sauce
1 cans Rotel Tomatoes
2 C. water
1 packages taco seasoning mix

1 package ranch dressing mix
sour cream
grated cheese
picante sauce or Tabasco sauce
sliced jalapeno
green onion
crushed tortilla chips

Directions
1. Drain the all the beans with corn and rinse them.
2. Stir them into a large soup pot with the remaining ingredients. Put on the lid and let them cook for 40 to 60 min.
3. Serve your navy taco soup hot.
4. Enjoy.

Tacos Gonzalez

Prep Time: 30 mins
Total Time: 50 mins

Servings per Recipe: 6
Calories   841.2
Fat   42.6g
Cholesterol   169.0mg
Sodium   2015.3mg
Carbohydrates   59.1g
Protein   58.1g

Ingredients
1 1/2 lbs steak
6 garlic cloves, mashed with
1 tsp kosher salt
3/4 C. fresh orange juice
2 tbsp tequila, optional
2 tbsp ground red chili pepper
1 C. chopped fresh cilantro
1 tbsp chopped fresh oregano
2 tsp salt
1 tbsp fresh coarse ground black pepper
1/4 C. olive oil
24 corn tortillas
1 lb queso asadero cheese
6 fire poblano chiles
guacamole
salsa, of your choice
1 large red onion, thinly sliced
1/4 C. fresh lime juice
1 tbsp olive oil
1/2 tsp salt
2 tbsp chopped fresh cilantro
1 tsp chopped fresh oregano

Directions
1. Get a mixing bowl: Mix in it the orange tequila, orange juice, garlic, chili pepper, cilantro, oregano, oil, salt and pepper to make the marinade.
2. Use a sharp knife to pose the steak several times. Place it in a plastic bag and pour the marinade all over it.
3. Seal the bag and place the steak in the fridge for an overnight.
4. Get a zip lock bag. Place in it the red onion with lime juice, olive oil, cilantro, oregano and salt.
5. Seal the bag and place it in the fridge of 3 h to 4 days to make the pickled onion.
6. Before you do anything, preheat the grill and grease it.
7. Drain the steak then season it with some salt and pepper. Grill it for 4 to 7 min on each side or until it is done to your taste.
8. Wrap the steak in a piece of foil then place it aside.
9. Heat the tortillas in a pan. Lay 2 slices of cheese on a tortilla then fold it in half then wrap each one of them in a piece of foil.
10. Place them over the grill and cook them for 10 to 14 min until the cheese slightly melts.
11. Cut the steak into thin slices. Place them over the cheese layer.
12. Top it with fire roasted chile, pickled onions, guacamole and salsa.
13. Fold the tortillas over the filling. Serve your tacos right away.
14. Enjoy.

EAST LA
Refried Casserole

Prep Time: 15 mins
Total Time: 30 mins

Servings per Recipe: 8
Calories   239.1
Fat   18.4g
Cholesterol   53.6mg
Sodium   467.7mg
Carbohydrates   12.2g
Protein   7.3g

Ingredients

1 cans refried beans
1 packages cream cheese, softened
1 C. sour cream
2 tbsp taco seasoning mix
2 cloves garlic, pressed
2 oz. cheddar cheese, shredded
1 can pitted ripe olives

1 medium tomatoes, seeded and chopped
2 green onions, chopped
fresh cilantro, chopped
tortilla chips

Directions

1. Before you do anything, preheat the oven to 350. Grease a casserole dish with a cooking spray.
2. Spread in it the refried beans. Cream cheese, sour cream, taco seasoning, and garlic. Beat them until they become smooth.
3. Pour the mix all over the beans layer. Top it with the cheddar cheese, olives, tomato, onion and cilantro.
4. Place the dip in the oven and cook it for 16 min. serve it hot.
5. Enjoy.

Whole Wheat Tacos

Prep Time: 15 mins
Total Time: 17 mins

Servings per Recipe: 4
Calories	652.3
Fat	34.1g
Cholesterol	123.9mg
Sodium	1413.5mg
Carbohydrates	41.5g
Protein	43.1g

Ingredients

- 1 lb lean ground beef
- 1/2 C. chopped onion
- 1 clove garlic, minced or pressed
- 1 tsp salt
- 1/2 tsp chili powder
- 2 C. shredded Monterey jack cheese
- 1 C. diced tomato
- 1 C. diced jalapenos
- 4 large wheat flour tortillas
- oil, for frying

Directions

1. Place a large pan over medium heat. Cook in it the meat with garlic and onion for 8 min. discard the fat.
2. Stir in the chili powder and salt to make the filling.
3. Place a tortilla on a working surface. Top one half of it with 1/2 C. of the ground beef filling, 1/2 C. of cheese, and 1/2 C. of tomatoes and some chilies.
4. Fold the second half over the filling and press it. Repeat the process with the remaining ingredients to make 3 more tortillas.
5. Place a large skillet over medium heat. Heat the oil in it. Cook in it the stuffed tortillas for 2 to 3 min on each side.
6. Serve your tacos warm your favorite toppings.
7. Enjoy.

SONOMA
Chicken Tacos

Prep Time: 20 mins
Total Time: 50 mins

Servings per Recipe: 4
Calories   477.5
Fat   12.5g
Cholesterol   115.2mg
Sodium   1104.6mg
Carbohydrates   43.7g
Protein   44.9g

Ingredients
1 1/2 lbs boneless skinless chicken breasts, cubed
1/8 C. red vinegar
1/2 lime, juice of
1 tsp white sugar
1/2 tsp salt
1/2 tsp ground black pepper
2 green onions, chopped
2 cloves garlic, minced
1 tsp dried oregano
10 6-inch flour tortillas

1 tomatoes, diced
1/4 C. shredded lettuce
1/4 C. shredded Monterey jack cheese
1/4 C. salsa

Directions
1. Place a large saucepan over medium heat. Heat in it a splash of oil. Cook in it the chicken pieces with a pinch of salt for 22 min over low heat.
2. Stir in the vinegar, lime juice, sugar, salt, pepper, green onion, garlic and oregano. Cook them for 12 min.
3. Place a large pan over medium heat. Heat in it the tortillas.
4. Place the tortillas on serving plates. Place the chicken filling on top followed by tomato, lettuce, cheese and salsa.
5. Serve your tacos right away.
6. Enjoy.

Barcelona Shrimp Tacos

🍲 Prep Time: 15 mins
🕒 Total Time: 30 mins

Servings per Recipe: 1
Calories 755.9
Fat 19.4g
Cholesterol 478.2mg
Sodium 3097.5mg
Carbohydrates 89.5g
Protein 63.1g

Ingredients

- 1 C. tomatoes, chopped
- 1 C. avocado, diced
- 1/2 C. cilantro, chopped
- 3/4 tsp salt
- 1/4 tsp black pepper
- 1 lb cooked shrimp, peeled
- 1 jalapeno, chopped
- 1 garlic clove, chopped
- 12 corn tortillas
- 1/4 C. lime juice
- 1 tbsp of lime zest, grated

Directions

1. Get a mixing bowl: Toss in all the ingredients.
2. Place a large pan over medium heat. Heat in it the tortillas.
3. Place the tortillas on serving plates. Top them with the shrimp mix.
4. Fold the tortillas over the filling then serve them with your favorite toppings.
5. Enjoy.

AFTER-SCHOOL
Pasta Tacos

Prep Time: 40 mins
Total Time: 1 hrs

Servings per Recipe: 12
Calories   370.3
Fat   16.4g
Cholesterol   63.9mg
Sodium   444.1mg
Carbohydrates   33.7g
Protein   23.1g

Ingredients
10 oz. dried spaghetti, broken
2 lbs ground beef
2 large onions, chopped
1 1/2 C. water
1 envelopes taco seasoning mix
2 cans corn, drained
1 1/2 C. colby-monterey jack cheese, shredded
1 C. salsa
2 cans diced green chili peppers, drained
4 C. lettuce, shredded
1 medium tomatoes, chopped

Directions
1. Before you do anything, preheat the oven to 375 F. Grease 2 baking dishes.
2. Prepare the noodles by following the instructions on the package.
3. Place a large pot over medium heat. Stir in it the onion with meat and cook them for 12 min. discard the fat.
4. Mix in it the seasoning mix with water. Cook them until they start boiling. Lower the heat and let them cook for 3 min.
5. Fold the noodles into the sauce mix with corn, 1 C. of the shredded cheese, salsa and chili peppers.
6. Spoon the mixture into the greased dishes. Cover them with a piece of oil. Cook them in the oven for 22 to 26 min.
7. Discard the foil then top them with the cheese, lettuce and tomato. Serve it hot.
8. Enjoy.

Lorna's Bruschetta Mexicana

Prep Time: 20 mins
Total Time: 35 mins

Servings per Recipe: 4
Calories 291.4
Fat 18.4g
Cholesterol 113.8mg
Sodium 966.5mg
Carbohydrates 24.7g
Protein 9.0g

Ingredients

- 1/2 C. can corn, drained
- 1/2 C. can black beans, rinsed and drained
- 2 tbsp red bell peppers, minced
- 2 tbsp green onions, minced
- 1/4 C. tomato, minced
- 1/4 tsp cumin
- 1/2 tsp sugar
- 1 1/4 tsp salt
- 3/8 tsp black pepper
- 2 tbsp white vinegar
- 2 tbsp canola oil
- 1/2 tsp canola oil
- 1 packages Hash Browns
- 1 garlic clove, crushed
- 3 tbsp chopped cilantro
- 1/3 C. yellow onion, minced
- 2 1/2 tsp packaged taco seasoning mix
- 2 large eggs
- 1/4 C. flour
- 2 tbsp butter
- 1 oz. goat cheese, crumbled

Directions

1. Get a mixing bowl: Mix in it the corn, black beans, red bell peppers, green onions and tomato.
2. Mix in the cumin, sugar, 1/4 t. kosher salt, and 1/8 tsp of black pepper, vinegar and 1/2 tsp of canola oil. Place it aside.
3. Get another mixing bowl: Mix in it the hash brown potatoes, garlic, 2 tbsp cilantro, yellow onion, taco seasoning, remaining 1 tsp kosher salt and 1/4 tsp black pepper.
4. Mix in the flour with eggs.
5. Place a large skillet over medium heat. Heat in it 1 tbsp of butter and 1 tbsp of oil.
6. Drop 6 cakes of the mixture using 2 tbsp for each cake. Cook them for 4 to 6 min until they become golden brown on each side.
7. Drain the potato cakes and place them aside. Heat another tbsp of oil and butter in the pan then repeat the process with the remaining mixture.
8. Serve your potato taco cakes right away with the beans salad and some goat cheese.
9. Enjoy.

PINWHEEL
Taco

Prep Time: 30 mins
Total Time: 55 mins

Servings per Recipe: 20
Calories	97.6
Fat	7.1g
Cholesterol	27.2mg
Sodium	228.3mg
Carbohydrates	1.1g
Protein	7.0g

Ingredients
1 lb ground beef
1 envelopes taco seasoning mix
2/3 C. water
1 lb frozen bread dough, thawed
2 C. grated cheddar cheese

Directions
1. Before you do anything, preheat the oven to 350 F. Line up 2 baking sheets with some parchment paper.
2. Place a large pan over medium heat. Cook in it the beef with water and taco seasoning for 8 to 12 min.
3. Place the dough on a slightly floured surface. Spread it in the shape of a 20 inches rectangle.
4. Lay the cooked beef on top in an even layer, while leaving the edges empty. Roll the dough over the filling and press the edges to seal them.
5. Use a sharp knife to slice the roll into slightly thick slices. Place in it the dough slices and cook them for 26 min until they become golden brown.
6. Serve your taco wheels right away with your favorite toppings.
7. Enjoy.

Skinny Hot Fish Tacos

Prep Time: 15 mins
Total Time: 25 mins

Servings per Recipe: 4
Calories 259.6
Fat 12.4g
Cholesterol 52.1mg
Sodium 561.7mg
Carbohydrates 13.5g
Protein 25.5g

Ingredients
1 lb salmon, cubed
1 tbsp cumin
1 tsp chili powder
2 tbsp olive oil
1 medium yellow onion, chopped
2 limes, quartered
2 cans diced tomatoes with green chilies, drained
1/2 bunch fresh cilantro, chopped
1 bunch green onion, chopped

Directions
1. Get a mixing bowl: Stir in it the salmon with cumin, chili powder, a pinch of salt and pepper.
2. Place a large pan over medium heat. Heat the oil in it. Add the onion and cook it for 3 min.
3. Stir in the salmon then cook them over high heat for 3 to 4 min.
4. Place the salmon in the tortillas then top them with salsa, sour cream, sliced avocado, and crisp romaine lettuce.
5. Serve your tacos right away.
6. Enjoy.

GARDEN
Party Tacos

Prep Time: 30 mins
Total Time: 45 mins

Servings per Recipe: 12
Calories   304.8
Fat   14.2g
Cholesterol   51.4mg
Sodium   586.4mg
Carbohydrates   23.9g
Protein   19.3g

Ingredients

2 lbs ground beef
3 tbsp taco seasoning mix
6 oz. tomato sauce
20 1/2 oz. refried beans
shredded cheddar cheese
12 small flour tortillas
diced tomato

diced onion
sour cream
salsa
shredded lettuce

Directions

1. Before you do anything, preheat the oven to 375 F. Grease a casserole dish.
2. Place a large pan over medium heat. Cook in it the beef for 8 min. discard the fat.
3. Mix in the taco seasoning, refried beans and tomato sauce. Cook them for 2 min.
4. Divide the beef mixture between the tortillas then lay them in the casserole dish. Sprinkle over it the cheese.
5. Place the casserole in the oven and cook it for 16 min.
6. Garnish your casserole with some tomato, onion, sour cream, salsa and lettuce.
7. Enjoy.

Spicy Jalapeno Potato Tacos

Prep Time: 30 mins
Total Time: 55 mins

Servings per Recipe: 4
Calories 242.8
Fat 5.1g
Cholesterol 9.0mg
Sodium 273.5mg
Carbohydrates 43.4g
Protein 7.4g

Ingredients
- 2 whole jalapeno peppers, minced
- 12 corn tortillas
- 2 C. boiled potatoes, mashed
- 2 tbsp taco seasoning mix
- 1/2 C. shredded cheese
- 1/4 C. fresh cilantro, minced
- cooking oil

Directions
1. Get a mixing bowl: Mix in it the cilantro with mashed potato, taco seasoning, cheese, a pinch of salt and pepper.
2. Heat the tortillas in a pan for 1 to 2 min on each side.
3. Spread 1 tbsp of potato filling on each tortilla then roll it tightly. Place them in a greased baking dish.
4. Transfer the tacos to the freezer and let them sit for 16 min.
5. Place a large pan over medium heat. Heat in it some oil. Add 4 tacos and cook them for 2 to 3 min on each side until they become golden brown.
6. Repeat the process with the remaining tacos. Serve them with your favorite toppings.
7. Enjoy.

MESSY Shrimp Tacos with Cilantro Dressing

Prep Time: 20 mins
Total Time: 35 mins

Servings per Recipe: 4
Calories   578.4
Fat   33.1g
Cholesterol   189.9mg
Sodium   1706.0mg
Carbohydrates   47.6g
Protein   27.0g

Ingredients
12 corn tortillas
2 tbsp vegetable oil
1 package Simply Potatoes Diced Potatoes with Onion
1 C. sour cream
1 envelopes taco seasoning mix
4 tbsp fresh squeezed lime juice, divided
1/2 C. chopped fresh cilantro, divided
1/4 tsp salt
1 lb fresh medium shrimp, shelled and deveined, tails removed
1/2 tsp ground cumin
3 green onions, chopped
1 C. fresh Baby Spinach, ribbons
1 large tomatoes, diced
1 Hass avocado, diced
3 oz. crumbled goat cheese

Directions
1. Before you do anything, preheat the oven to 250 F.
2. Place a large pan over medium heat. Heat in it the oil. Cook in it the potatoes with onion for 11 min with the lid on while stirring them often.
3. Get a blender: Combine in it the sour cream, about ½ of the taco seasoning, 2 tbsp lime juice, half of the chopped cilantro and the salt.
4. Blend them smooth to make the dressing.
5. Get a mixing bowl: Stir in it the shrimp with taco seasoning, cumin, a pinch of salt and pepper.
6. Add them to the potato pan and cook them for 4 to 6 min. Spoon the mixture into the tortillas.
7. Top them with some spinach, tomato, avocado, goat cheese, and cilantro dressing.
8. Serve your tacos right away.
9. Enjoy.

Mexican
Lunch Box Fries

Prep Time:	10 mins
Total Time:	15 mins

Servings per Recipe: 6
Calories   188.3
Fat   4.6g
Cholesterol   0.0mg
Sodium   529.4mg
Carbohydrates   33.6g
Protein   3.1g

Ingredients
2 tbsp taco seasoning mix
1 bags frozen crispy French fries

Directions
1. Before you do anything, preheat the oven to 350 F. Line up a baking sheet with parchment paper.
2. Lay in it the French fries. Cook them in the oven for 14 min.
3. Season the fries with taco seasoning then serve them right away.
4. Enjoy.

ALAMEDA
Tacos with Onion Flakes

Prep Time: 5 mins
Total Time: 15 mins

Servings per Recipe: 5
Calories   255.8
Fat   10.5g
Cholesterol   30.8mg
Sodium   685.2mg
Carbohydrates   26.6g
Protein   12.7g

Ingredients

1/2 lb ground beef
2 tbsp flour
3/4 tsp salt
1/4 tsp dried onion flakes
1/4 tsp paprika
1 1/2 tsp chili powder
1 dash garlic powder
1 dash onion powder
1/4 C. water
5 small tortillas
lettuce

shredded cheese
sour cream
tomatoes, diced

Directions

1. Get a mixing bowl: Mix in it the beef with the flour, salt, minced onion, paprika, chili powder, garlic powder and onion powder.
2. Place a large pan over medium heat. Cook in it the beef mixture with water for 10 to 12 min or until the beef is done.
3. Heat the tortillas in a pan then top them with the beef mixture followed by tomato, lettuce, cheese and sour cream.
4. Serve your tacos right away.
5. Enjoy.

Rust Belt Tacos

Prep Time: 10 mins
Total Time: 10 mins

Servings per Recipe: 4	
Calories	666.4
Fat	26.7g
Cholesterol	106.7mg
Sodium	991.1mg
Carbohydrates	71.6g
Protein	36.0g

Ingredients
- 1 lb ground beef
- 1 envelopes taco seasoning mix
- 4 large hot baked potatoes
- 1 C. cheddar cheese
- 1 C. chopped green onion
- salsa
- sour cream

Directions
1. Place a large pan over medium heat. Cook in it the beef for 8 to 10 min or until it is done. Discard the grease.
2. Mix in the taco seasoning by following the instructions on the package.
3. Make 2 crossing slices on top of each potatoes in the shape of an X. Use a fork to fluff the potato flesh slightly.
4. Divide the beef between the potatoes then place them on a serving plate.
5. Top them with cheese, green onion and some sour cream. Serve them right away.
6. Enjoy.

KATRINA'S
Mesa Lasagna

Prep Time: 20 mins
Total Time: 50 mins

Servings per Recipe: 4
Calories   1154.6
Fat   44.8g
Cholesterol   103.9mg
Sodium   3411.2mg
Carbohydrates   139.7g
Protein   49.7g

Ingredients

1 lb ground beef round
1/2 C. chopped green pepper
1/2 C. chopped onion
2/3 C. water
1 envelopes taco seasoning
1 cans black beans
1 cans petite diced tomatoes

6 large flour tortillas
1 cans refried beans
3- 4 C. Mexican blend cheese
chopped fresh cilantro leaves
sour cream

Directions

1. Before you do anything, preheat the oven to 350 F. Grease a casserole dish.
2. Place a large pan over medium heat. Cook in it the beef with onion and green pepper for 8 min.
3. Stir in the water with taco seasoning. Cook them until they start boiling. Lower the heat and let them cook for an extra 6 min.
4. Add the tomatoes and black beans. Cook them for 12 min.
5. Lay 2 tortillas in the bottom of the casserole. Top it with half of the refried beans followed by half of the beef mixture, and 1 C. of shredded cheese.
6. Repeat the process to make another layer. Cover the second layer with the remaining tortillas and cheese.
7. Use a piece of foil to cover the casserole. Cook it in the oven for 32 min. serve it warm with your favorite toppings.
8. Enjoy.

Creamy Sirloin and Pasta Taco Casserole

Prep Time: 10 mins
Total Time: 30 mins

Servings per Recipe: 6
Calories   547.9
Fat   23.8g
Cholesterol   99.1mg
Sodium   1088.9mg
Carbohydrates   48.9g
Protein   34.0g

Ingredients

- 1 lb ground sirloin
- 1 small onion, chopped
- 16 oz. can tomato sauce
- 16 oz. can water
- 16 oz. can diced tomatoes and green chilies, undrained
- 3 C. uncooked elbow macaroni
- 1/4 tsp salt
- 1/4 tsp pepper
- 1/2-1 tsp cumin
- 1/8-1/4 tsp cayenne pepper
- 1/2 tsp garlic powder
- 1 tsp dried cilantro
- 1/2 C. milk
- 2-2 1/2 C. shredded cheddar cheese

Directions

1. Place a large pan over medium heat. Cook in it the sirloin with onion for 8 min. discard the grease.
2. Mix in it the tomato sauce, water, diced tomatoes, dry macaroni and seasonings. Cook them until they start boiling.
3. Lower the heat and put on the lid. Let them cook for 14 to 16 min.
4. Stir in the milk with cheese and cook them for 4 min. serve your sirloin and pasta taco casserole warm with your favorite toppings.
5. Enjoy.

MI LINDA'S Tacos

Prep Time: 7 mins
Total Time: 1 hr 7 mins

Servings per Recipe: 5
Calories   271.6
Fat   9.6g
Cholesterol   58.9mg
Sodium   276.9mg
Carbohydrates   21.6g
Protein   24.8g

Ingredients
1 lb ground beef
1 cans black beans
1 cans stewed tomatoes, chopped
1 envelopes taco seasoning mix
1 envelope ranch dressing mix

Directions
1. Place a large pan over medium heat. Cook in it the beef for 8 min. discard the grease.
2. Stir in the beans with tomatoes, taco seasoning and ranch dressing mix. Put on the lid and cook them for 1 h on low heat.
3. Spoon the filling into the taco shells.
4. Serve your tacos right away with your favorite toppings.
5. Enjoy.

Carolina Cornbread Taco Casserole

Prep Time: 15 mins
Total Time: 40 mins

Servings per Recipe: 4
Calories 666.8
Fat 29.2g
Cholesterol 88.2mg
Sodium 1677.5mg
Carbohydrates 72.3g
Protein 32.1g

Ingredients
- 1 lb ground beef
- 1 package taco seasoning mix
- 1/2 C. water
- 1 cans corn, drained
- 1/2 C. green pepper, chopped
- 1 cans tomato sauce
- 1 packages Jiffy cornbread mix
- 1 cans French-fried onions
- 1/3 C. shredded cheddar cheese

Directions
1. Before you do anything, preheat the oven to 400 F. Grease a baking dish.
2. Place a large pan over medium heat. Cook in it the beef for 8 min. discard the grease.
3. Mix in the taco seasoning, water, corn, green pepper and tomato sauce.
4. Prepare the cornbread mixture by following the instructions on the package. Mix into it half of the fried onions.
5. Pour the beef mixture into the greased casserole. Top it with the cornbread mix.
6. Cook it in the oven for 22 min. garnish the casserole with cheese and the remaining onion. Cook it for an extra 3 min.
7. Serve your taco bake right away with your favorite toppings.
8. Enjoy.

CHILI Taco Ranch Wheels

Prep Time: 20 mins
Total Time: 1 hr 50 mins

Servings per Recipe: 24
Calories   223.5
Fat   10.6g
Cholesterol   20.8mg
Sodium   517.3mg
Carbohydrates   26.8g
Protein   5.2g

Ingredients
2 packages cream cheese, softened
1 cans chopped green chilies, drained
1 cans chopped black olives, drained
1/4 C. pimiento, drained
1 packages taco seasoning mix
1 package dry ranch dressing mix
10 - 12 large flour tortillas

Directions
1. Get a mixing bowl: Combine in it the cream cheese with chilies, olives, pimiento, seasoning mix, and ranch dressing to make the filling.
2. Place a large pan over medium heat. Divide the filling between the tortillas and spread it.
3. Roll the tortillas over the filling. Place them in the fridge for 2 h.
4. Once the time is up, use a sharp knife to slice the tortillas into slices. Serve them with your favorite toppings.
5. Enjoy.

Taco Bites

Prep Time: 30 mins
Total Time: 45 mins

Servings per Recipe: 16
Calories 488.2
Fat 33.4g
Cholesterol 49.9mg
Sodium 332.7mg
Carbohydrates 31.1g
Protein 15.7g

Ingredients

- 2 packages puff pastry sheets
- 1 egg
- 1/2 tbsp water
- 1 1/2 lbs ground beef
- 1/2 C. green pepper, chopped
- 1/2 C. white onion, chopped
- 1 garlic clove, minced
- 1 medium tomatoes, seeded and chopped
- 1/2 C. catsup
- 1/4 C. fresh cilantro
- 1 tsp ground cumin
- 2 tsp chili powder
- 1 tsp oregano
- 1 tsp cinnamon
- 1 1/2 C. Monterey jack cheese, shredded

Directions

1. Before you do anything, preheat the oven to 375 F. Line up a baking sheet with parchment paper.
2. Place the pastry on a working surface to defrost for 35 min.
3. Place a large pan over medium heat. Cook in it the beef, onion and green pepper for 4 min. Stir in the garlic and cook them for an extra minute..
4. Discard the grease from the pan. Mix in the tomato, catsup, cilantro or parsley, cumin, chili powder, oregano and cinnamon.
5. Lower the heat and let them cook for 11 min. turn off the heat and add the cheese to make the filling. Place it aside to cool down.
6. Lay the pastry into a rectangle then slice it into 8 slices. Place 1 tsp of the filling in the middle of each dough piece.
7. Get a small mixing bowl: Whisk in it the egg with water. Use the mixture to brush the pastry edges.
8. Pull one corner of the dough over the filling and press it onto the opposite corner in a triangle shape.
9. Repeat the process with the remaining ingredients. Place them on the lined up pan and brush them completely with the remaining egg and water mix.
10. Cook them in the oven for 16 to 18 min until they become golden brown. Serve your taco bites with your favorite dipping sauce.
11. Enjoy.

MESA
Cod Tacos

Prep Time: 10 mins
Total Time: 55 mins

Servings per Recipe: 6
Calories 221.9
Fat 4.0g
Cholesterol 53.7mg
Sodium 94.6mg
Carbohydrates 23.0g
Protein 23.4g

Ingredients
1 1/4 C. Lawry Baja chipotle marinade, with lime juice
1 1/2 lbs cod
1/4 C. mayonnaise
1/4 C. sour cream
12 soft corn tortillas, warmed
2 C. green cabbage, shredded

Directions
1. Get a zip lock bag. Place a large pan over medium heat. Place in it the cod fillets. Add to them 3/4 C. of the Baja marinade.
2. Seal the bag and place it in the fridge for 32 min.
3. Before you do anything else, preheat the grill and grease it.
4. Drain the fish fillets and cook them for 3 to 5 min on each side until they are done. Baste the fish while it is cooking with 1/4 C. of the marinade.
5. Get a small mixing bowl: Whisk in it the mayonnaise, sour cream, and the remaining of marinade.
6. Place the fish fillets in the taco shells. Drizzle over them the dressing and top them with your favorite toppings.
7. Enjoy.

Italian Tacos with Tortilla Chips

Prep Time: 25 mins
Total Time: 45 mins

Servings per Recipe: 4
Calories	999.4
Fat	63.8g
Cholesterol	45.9mg
Sodium	1988.5mg
Carbohydrates	86.4g
Protein	33.6g

Ingredients

- 12 corn tortillas
- 1/2 tsp sea salt, ground, divided
- 8 oz. mild Italian chicken sausage, casings removed
- 1 jar tomato sauce, divided
- 1 cans black beans, drained
- 1 tsp chili powder
- 1 tsp ground cumin
- 1/2 tsp garlic powder
- 1/2 tsp onion powder
- 1/4 tsp cayenne pepper
- 4 avocados, mashed
- 2 spring onions, sliced
- 3/4 C. cilantro, chopped, divided
- 2 jalapeno peppers, minced
- 2 garlic cloves, minced
- 2 tbsp lime juice
- 1/4 tsp ground black pepper
- 1 packages pine nuts
- 4 C. arugula
- 4 tbsp sour cream
- 1/4 C. sharp cheddar cheese, shredded

Directions

1. Before you do anything, preheat the oven to 350 F. Grease a cookie sheet with oil.
2. Slice the tortillas into 6 strips.
3. Lay the tortillas strips on the cookie sheet. Grease them with a cooking spray then season them with 1/4 tsp of sea salt.
4. Place a large pan over medium heat. Cook in it the sausages for 8 min. discard the fat.
5. Reserve 1/2 C. of the ragu sauce. Stir the remaining sauce into the sausage pan with black beans, chili powder, cumin, garlic powder, onion powder and crushed red pepper.
6. Bring them to a boil while stirring them often.
7. Get a mixing bowl: Mix in it the avocados, reserved 1/2 C. Ragu sauce, spring onions, 1/2 C. cilantro, jalapeno peppers, minced garlic, lime juice, salt, black pepper and pine nuts.
8. Lay 1 C. of arugula on each serving plate then top it with the sausage mixture followed by the avocado sauce, 1 tbsp of sour cream, cheese, and 1/4 C. of cilantro.
9. Serve your taco plates with the tortilla chips.
10. Enjoy.

STATE
Fair Tacos

Prep Time: 5 mins
Total Time: 20 mins

Servings per Recipe: 12
Calories   412.9
Fat   15.8g
Cholesterol   41.2mg
Sodium   670.0mg
Carbohydrates   46.8g
Protein   20.2g

Ingredients

12 frozen dinner rolls
1 lb ground beef
1 package taco seasoning mix
2 C. chopped lettuce
1 tomatoes, chopped
2 C. shredded cheese

Directions

1. Place the frozen rolls aside to defrost and rise until it doubles in size.
2. Place a large pan over medium heat. Cook it the beef for 8 min. discard the grease.
3. Mix in it the taco seasoning with 1/4 C. of water.
4. Place a deep pan over medium heat. Heat 2 inches of oil in it.
5. Place the dough rolls on a floured surface until they become thin. Cook them in the hot oil for 2 to 4 min on each side until they become golden brown.
6. Drain the taco rolls and place them on serving plates. Top them with the beef mixture, lettuce, tomato and cheese.
7. Serve your tacos right away with your other favorite toppings.
8. Enjoy.

Wednesday's Ground Beef Skillet

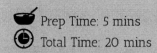

Prep Time: 5 mins
Total Time: 20 mins

Servings per Recipe: 5
Calories   380.9
Fat   14.5g
Cholesterol   61.6mg
Sodium   380.8mg
Carbohydrates   41.6g
Protein   22.2g

Ingredients
1 lb ground beef
1 envelopes taco seasoning mix
1 1/2 C. water
1 C. salsa
1 C. frozen whole kernel corn
1 1/2 C. uncooked instant rice

3/4 C. shredded taco blend cheese
1 C. shredded lettuce
1 medium tomatoes, chopped
sour cream

Directions
1. Place a large pan over medium heat. Brown in it the beef for 9 min. discard the grease.
2. Mix in it the seasoning mix, water, salsa and corn. Bring them to a boil. Mix in the rice and cook them for an extra minute.
3. Turn off the heat, put on the lid and let them sit for 9 min. Stir in the cheese.
4. Put on the lid again and let it sit for 2 min until the cheese melts.
5. Garnish your taco skillet with some tomato, lettuce, and sour cream.
6. Enjoy.

CON QUESO
Taco Bake

Prep Time: 5 mins
Total Time: 1 hr 5 mins

Servings per Recipe: 4
Calories 483.0
Fat 26.2g
Cholesterol 77.1mg
Sodium 1735.5mg
Carbohydrates 40.0g
Protein 24.7g

Ingredients
1 lb ground beef
1 packages taco seasoning
1/4 C. water
1/2 medium onion, diced

1 cans whole kernel corn
1 jars salsa con queso
1/2 lb tater tots

Directions
1. Before you do anything, preheat the oven to 350 F. Grease a baking dish.
2. Place a large pan over medium heat. Cook in it the onion with beef for 9 min. discard the grease.
3. Mix in the taco seasoning with water. Cook them for 2 min.
4. Spoon the mixture into the greased dish in an even layer. Top them with the tater tots followed by corn and salsa.
5. Place the dish in the oven and let it cook for 60 min. serve it hot.
6. Enjoy.

Ciudad Tacos

Prep Time: 5 mins
Total Time: 20 mins

Servings per Recipe: 4
Calories   815.7
Fat   15.9g
Cholesterol   0.0mg
Sodium   2463.5mg
Carbohydrates   142.9g
Protein   25.0g

Ingredients
2 cans garbanzo beans
1 packets taco seasoning
10 tortillas

Directions
1. Drain the garbanzo beans and reserve 1 can liquid. Rinse the beans under some cool water and drain it again.
2. Place a large pan over medium heat. Stir in it the garbanzo liquid with the rinsed beans, and taco seasoning.
3. Cook them for 12 to 14 min. Use a potato masher to press 1/4 of the bean mixture.
4. Spoon the mixture into the taco shells then serve them right away with your favorite toppings.
5. Enjoy.

SAUCY BEEF
Taco Casserole

Prep Time: 30 mins
Total Time: 1 hr

Servings per Recipe: 4
Calories   522.0
Fat   31.2g
Cholesterol   125.0mg
Sodium   1484.4mg
Carbohydrates   23.1g
Protein   37.1g

Ingredients
- 8 oz. medium egg noodles, cooked and drained
- 1 lb ground beef, cooked, drained
- 1/2 C. chopped onion, cooked, drained
- 1 cans tomato sauce
- 1/2 C. water
- 1 packets taco seasoning mix
- 16 oz. cottage cheese
- 1/4 C. sour cream
- 1 tbsp flour
- 2 tsp beef bouillon granules
- 1/4 C. chopped green onion
- 1 cans diced green chilies
- 2 C. shredded Mexican blend cheese

Directions
1. Before you do anything, preheat the oven to 350 F. Grease a casserole dish.
2. Get a mixing bowl: Mix in it the cottage cheese, sour cream, flour, and beef bouillon. Stir into it the noodles with green onions and chilies.
3. Place a large deep skillet over medium heat. Brown in it the beef with onion for 9 min.
4. Mix in the tomato sauce, water and taco seasoning. Cook them for 12 min.
5. Pour the noodles mixture into the greased casserole. Top it with the beef mixture followed by cheese.
6. Place the casserole in the oven and cook it for 26 to 32 min.
7. Serve your taco casserole warm with your favorite toppings.
8. Enjoy.

Mexican Popcorn

Prep Time: 5 mins
Total Time: 5 mins

Servings per Recipe: 4
Calories   166.9
Fat   18.3g
Cholesterol   30.5mg
Sodium   154.8mg
Carbohydrates   1.1g
Protein   0.2g

Ingredients
1/2 C. popcorn
2 tbsp oil
1/4 C. butter

1 tbsp taco seasoning
salt, if desired

Directions
1. Place a large pot over high heat. Heat in it the oil with corn kernels.
2. Put on the lid and let them cook until the corn start popping. Shake the pot and let the popcorn cook until the popcorn stop popping.
3. Melt the butter in the microwave. Mix into it the taco seasoning. Add it to the popcorn and toss them to coat.
4. Serve your taco popcorn warm.
5. Enjoy.

REFRIED
Taco Pizza

Prep Time: 30 mins
Total Time: 45 mins

Servings per Recipe: 1
Calories	1336.0
Fat	80.3g
Cholesterol	272.8mg
Sodium	3995.0mg
Carbohydrates	69.1g
Protein	86.0g

Ingredients
1 lb ground beef
1 envelopes taco seasoning
1 C. water
2 prebaked prepared pizza crust
1 cans refried beans
3/4 C. salsa
2 C. coarsely crushed tortilla chips
2 C. shredded cheddar cheese
2 medium tomatoes, chopped
1 C. shredded lettuce

Directions
1. Before you do anything, preheat the oven to 350 F. Grease a pizza pan.
2. Place a heavy saucepan over medium heat. Cook in it the beef for 10 min. discard the grease.
3. Mix in the water with taco seasoning. Cook them until they start boiling. Lower the heat and let them cook for 12 min over low heat.
4. Get a mixing bowl: Mix in it the salsa with refried beans.
5. Place the pizza crust on the pan. Spread it over it the beans mixture followed by the beef mixture, tortilla chips and cheese.
6. Place the pizza in the oven and cook it for 15 to 17 min. Garnish it with some tomato and lettuce then serve it.
7. Enjoy.

Mushroom Tacos

Prep Time: 20 mins
Total Time: 50 mins

Servings per Recipe: 4
Calories   296.4
Fat   10.5g
Cholesterol   0.0mg
Sodium   596.5mg
Carbohydrates   43.5g
Protein   9.3g

Ingredients
- 4 portabella mushrooms, sliced
- 2 tsp dried oregano
- 1 1/2 tbsp olive oil
- 3 zucchini, sliced
- 1 red onion, sliced
- 8 wheat flour tortillas
- 3/4 C. cheese, shredded
- 1/2 C. salsa

Directions
1. Before you do anything, preheat the oven to 350 F. Grease a baking pan.
2. Get a mixing bowl: Stir in it the mushrooms, oregano, oil, salt and pepper, zucchini sticks, and onion slices.
3. Spread the mixture in the greased pan. Cook it in the oven for 30 min while stirring it every 15 min.
4. Heat the tortillas in a pan then spoon the mushroom mix into them.
5. Top those with cheese and salsa then serve them right away.
6. Enjoy.

TACO Volcanoes

Prep Time: 10 mins
Total Time: 40 mins

Servings per Recipe: 4
Calories   370.9
Fat   18.4g
Cholesterol   30.2mg
Sodium   716.8mg
Carbohydrates   48.1g
Protein   5.3g

Ingredients

1/2 tsp garlic powder
1/4 tsp ground cumin
2 lbs large white potatoes, cubed
2 tbsp butter
2 tbsp olive oil
salt and pepper, to taste
1 1/4 C. cubed Velveeta cheese
1/4 C. of your favorite salsa

Tabasco sauce, to taste
1/2 C. sour cream, divided
1 green onion, chopped

Directions

1. Before you do anything, preheat the oven to 350 F. Grease a baking pan.
2. Get a mixing bowl: Toss in it the potato with cumin, garlic powder, potato and a pinch of salt.
3. Place a large pan over medium heat. Cook in it the potato mixture for 12 min while stirring it often. Put on the lid and let them cook for an extra 8 min over low heat.
4. Pour the mixture into the greased pan and spread it in an even layer. Cook it in the oven for 9 min while stirring it often.
5. Get a microwave safe bowl: Toss in it the Velveeta cheese, salsa, and Tabasco. Cook it in the microwave for 60 sec.
6. Mix it well and microwave it for another 60 sec then repeat the process a third time to make the sauce.
7. Spoon the crispy potato into serving plates. Top them with the cheese sauce.
8. Serve your taco plates right away with your favorite toppings.
9. Enjoy.

Chipotle Pollo Guisado Tacos

Prep Time: 20 mins
Total Time: 70 mins

Servings per Recipe: 1
Calories   396.3
Fat   19.3g
Cholesterol   188.8mg
Sodium   530.1mg
Carbohydrates   7.9g
Protein   46.1g

Ingredients
2 lbs boneless skinless chicken thighs
3/4 tsp kosher salt, plus more
kosher salt, to taste
3 medium tomatoes, diced
1/4 C. canned chipotle chile in adobo
3/4 tsp ground cumin
3/4 tsp garlic powder
3/4 tsp fresh ground black pepper

3 tbsp olive oil
1 large onion, diced
taco shell
shredded lettuce
diced tomato
shredded cheddar cheese

Directions
1. Place a heavy saucepan with salted water over high heat. Stir in the chicken and cook it until it starts simmering. Let it cook for 26 min.
2. Drain the chicken thighs and shred them. Discard the bones.
3. Get a food processor: Combine in them the tomatoes, chipotle sauce, cumin, garlic powder, 3/4 tsp pepper, 3/4 tsp salt, and 1 C. water. Blend them smooth.
4. Place a heavy saucepan over medium heat. Heat the oil in it. Cook in it the onion for 8 to 9 min.
5. Stir in the tomato mixture. Cook them until they start simmering. Fold the chicken into the sauce mix. Cook them for 16 min.
6. Adjust the seasoning of the shredded chicken. Spoon it into the taco shells then top them with your favorite toppings. Serve them right away.
7. Enjoy.

SANTIAGO
Taco Pan

 Prep Time: 10 mins
Total Time: 20 mins

Servings per Recipe: 4
Calories   524.3
Fat   28.2g
Cholesterol   106.7mg
Sodium   948.9mg
Carbohydrates   35.8g
Protein   33.0g

Ingredients
1 lb ground beef
1 C. shredded cheddar cheese
8 corn tortillas, chopped
1/2 C. water
1 cans tomato soup
1 C. chunky salsa

Directions
1. Place a large pan over medium heat. Cook in it the beef for 9 min. discard the fat.
2. Mix in the soup, salsa, water, tortillas, and half of cheese. Bring them to a boil.
3. Put on the lid and let them cook for 6 min. Stir in the remaining cheese until it melts then serve it hot with your favorite toppings.
4. Enjoy.

Manhattan Island Taco Bagels

Prep Time: 15 mins
Total Time: 35 mins

Servings per Recipe: 1
Calories 195.6
Fat 5.8g
Cholesterol 15.7mg
Sodium 393.2mg
Carbohydrates 26.9g
Protein 8.9g

Ingredients

10 miniature bagels, cut in half
2-3 C. cooked ground beef
1 green pepper, diced
1 red pepper, diced
1 onion, diced

10.5 oz. cheddar cheese, diced
2 tbsp taco seasoning
1/4 C. salsa

Directions

1. Before you do anything, preheat the oven to 350 F. Grease a baking pan.
2. Get a mixing bowl: Mix in it the beef with peppers, onion, cheese, salsa and taco seasoning.
3. Spoon the beef mixture over the bagels. Place them in the fridge for 24 min.
4. Cook the bagels in the oven for 24 to 26 min.
5. Serve your taco bagels right away with your favorite toppings.
6. Enjoy.

CLASSIC
Mac and Cheese Taco Casserole

Prep Time: 10 mins
Total Time: 20 mins

Servings per Recipe: 4
Calories   348.0
Fat   21.3g
Cholesterol   111.8mg
Sodium   1175.4mg
Carbohydrates   11.8g
Protein   26.7g

Ingredients

7 1/4 oz. Kraft macaroni and cheese
4 tbsp butter
1/4 C. skim milk
1 lb extra lean ground beef
1 packet taco seasoning
1 tbsp Louisiana hot sauce
1 tbsp butter

1 C. water
1 C. cheddar cheese

Directions

1. Prepare the mac and cheese by following the instructions on the package.
2. Place a large pan over medium heat. Cook in it the beef for 9 min. discard the fat.
3. Mix in the water with taco seasoning. Cook them for 6 min.
4. Stir in 1 tbsp of butter and 1 tbsp of hot sauce.
5. Drain the beef and stir into the mac and cheese with extra shredded cheese. Serve it hot.
6. Enjoy.

Spicy Skirt Tacos with Jalapeno Salsa and Lime Cream

🥣 Prep Time: 20 mins
🕐 Total Time: 40 mins

Servings per Recipe: 6
Calories   1415.6
Fat   93.9g
Cholesterol   211.8mg
Sodium   2618.8mg
Carbohydrates   78.0g
Protein   70.6g

Ingredients
3 1/2 lbs skirt steaks, strips
20 (4 inch) flour tortillas
1/2 C. canola oil
1 large napa cabbage, chopped
2 tsp dried chipotle powder
2 tbsp garlic powder
2 tbsp paprika
2 tbsp cumin
3 tsp kosher salt
1 jalapeno pepper
1 red onion, sliced
4 plum tomatoes
2 oz. canola oil
1 tsp kosher salt, kosher
1/2 bunch cilantro, chopped
3 limes, juice of, fresh
6 ripe Hass avocadoes, scooped
4 plum tomatoes, diced
1 red onion, minced,
1 bunch fresh cilantro, chopped
2 tsp salt, kosher
2 C. sour cream
2 fresh limes

Directions
1. Before you do anything, preheat the oven to 300 F. Heat in it the tortillas.
2. To prepare the steak:
3. Get a mixing bowl: Mix in it the spices. Add the steak and coat it with the spice mix.
4. Place a large pan over medium heat. Heat in it a drizzle of oil. Cook in it half of the steak mix for 3 to 4 min on each side.
5. Drain them and place them aside. Repeat the process with the remaining steak mixture.
6. To make the jalapeno salsa:
7. Place a large skillet over medium heat. Toss in it the jalapeño, onion, and tomatoes with a splash of oil. Cook them for 3 min while stirring them often.
8. Allow them to cool down for a while.
9. Get a blender: Place in it the veggies mix with a pinch of salt. Blend them smooth.
10. Get a large mixing bowl: Pour in it the puréed veggies. Stir in the cilantro and lime juice.
11. Cover the bowl with a plastic wrap. Place it in the fridge until ready to serve.

12. To make the Guacamole:
13. Get a mixing bowl: Mash in it the avocados. Mix into the tomatoes, red onion, cilantro, and salt. Place it in the fridge.
14. To make the lime cream:
15. Get a mixing bowl: Mix in it the sour cream with lime juice.
16. Serve your taco plates right away with your favorite toppings.
17. To assemble your tacos:
18. Lay 1/2 tbsp of guacamole on each tortilla, top it with some cabbage followed by the steak mixture. Fold the tortillas and place them over serving plates.
19. Top your tacos with the jalapeno salsa, guacamole and lime cream. Serve them right away.
20.   Enjoy.

Chipotle Taco Burgers

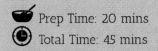

Prep Time: 20 mins
Total Time: 45 mins

Servings per Recipe: 4
Calories	310.8
Fat	19.1g
Cholesterol	125.3mg
Sodium	783.3mg
Carbohydrates	9.2g
Protein	24.9g

Ingredients

- 1 lb lean ground beef
- 1/2 C. of your favorite salsa
- 1 large egg
- 0.5 (1 1/4 oz.) package taco seasoning mix
- 1/3 C. mayonnaise
- 1 chipotle chile in adobo
- sliced tomatoes
- chopped fresh cilantro
- chopped red onion
- Monterey jack pepper cheese

Directions

1. Before you do anything, preheat the grill and grease it.
2. Get a mixing bowl: Mix in it the beef, 1/2 C. salsa, egg and the 1/2 packet of taco seasoning.
3. Divide the mix into 4 pieces and shape them into burgers. Place the burgers on the grill and cook them for 3 to 5 min on each side or until they are done.
4. Get a food processor: Blend it the mayonnaise with chipotle to make the dressing.
5. Place the burgers over heated tortillas then top them with some lettuce, onion, cilantro, and cheese and mayo sauce.
6. Serve your taco burger plates right away.
7. Enjoy.

TACO
Dip Morena

Prep Time: 20 mins
Total Time: 20 mins

Servings per Recipe: 10
Calories   419.6
Fat   30.8g
Cholesterol   42.5mg
Sodium   836.1mg
Carbohydrates   27.1g
Protein   12.9g

Ingredients
1 cans refried beans
3 ripe avocados
2 tbsp fresh lemon juice
1 tsp garlic salt
3-4 drops Tabasco sauce
1 1/4 C. sour cream
1/2 C. mayonnaise, plus
2 tbsp mayonnaise
1 packages taco seasoning mix
10-12 green onions, chopped
3 large tomatoes, chopped
2-3 C. black olives, sliced
2 C. cheddar cheese, shredded
corn chips

Directions
1. Get a large serving bowl: Lay in it the refried beans.
2. Get a mixing bowl: Mix in it the mashed avocado with lemon juice, garlic salt and tabasco.
3. Pour it all over the refried beans in an even layer.
4. Get a mixing bowl: Whisk in it the sour cream, mayonnaise and taco seasoning mix. Pour the mixture all over the avocado layer.
5. Top it with green onions, chopped tomatoes, olives and cheddar cheese.
6. Place the dip in the fridge until ready to serve.
7. Enjoy.

Taco Salad Madura's

Prep Time: 20 mins
Total Time: 30 mins

Servings per Recipe: 6
Calories   498.8
Fat   26.6g
Cholesterol   93.2mg
Sodium   881.1mg
Carbohydrates   33.2g
Protein   31.5g

Ingredients

1 lb ground beef
1 package taco seasoning mix
7 1/4 oz. packages nacho cheese tortilla chips, crushed
1 head iceberg lettuce, chopped
7 1/2 oz. cans kidney beans, drained
2 medium tomatoes, diced
3 green onions, sliced
2 C. shredded Mexican blend cheese
1/4 C. green goddess salad dressing

Directions

1. Place a large pan over medium heat. Heat in it a small splash of oil. Cook in it the beef for 9 min. discard the grease.
2. Mix in the taco seasoning mix by following the instructions on the package. Turn off the heat and let it cool down completely.
3. Lay the crushed chips in a serving bowl. Top it with the beef, cheese, beans, tomatoes, lettuce, and green onions.
4. Drizzle the dressing on top then serve your salad right away.
5. Enjoy.

ORANGE
Sirloin Tacos

Prep Time: 20 mins
Total Time: 30 mins

Servings per Recipe: 1
Calories	479.6
Fat	27.6g
Cholesterol	77.9mg
Sodium	639.1mg
Carbohydrates	31.8g
Protein	24.9g

Ingredients
- 20 oz. top sirloin steaks
- 1/4 C. orange juice
- 2 tbsp vegetable oil
- 1 tbsp lime juice
- 2 tsp cider vinegar
- 1/2 tsp dried oregano
- 1/2 tsp salt
- 1/4 tsp pepper
- 10 8-inch flour tortillas
- 2 1/2 C. shredded lettuce
- 1 1/4 C. finely shredded cheddar cheese
- 3/4 C. sour cream
- 2 small tomatoes, minced
- 1 bottles taco sauce

Directions
1. Get a mixing bowl: Mix in it the marinade ingredients.
2. Get a large roasting dish. Place in it the steaks and pour the marinade all over them.
3. Cover the steaks pan and place it in the fridge for 2 to 8 h. Let it sit for 1 h outside the fridge.
4. Before you do anything, preheat the grill and grease it.
5. Drain the steaks and cook them on the grill for 4 to 6 min on each side while basting them from time to time with the remaining marinade.
6. Cut the steaks into strips and place them aside.
7. Heat the tortillas in the microwave. Place the steak slices on the tortillas.
8. Top them with the 1/4 C. of lettuce, 2 tbsp cheese, 1 tbsp sour cream, a small amount of tomatoes and some taco sauce.
9. Serve your tacos right away.
10. Enjoy.

Grilled Halibut Tacos

Prep Time: 15 mins
Total Time: 25 mins

Servings per Recipe: 4
Calories   689.0
Fat   27.6g
Cholesterol   91.9mg
Sodium   1322.6mg
Carbohydrates   68.0g
Protein   46.0g

Ingredients

4 halibut steaks
olive oil
salt and pepper
1 lime, juiced
3 medium ripe Hass avocadoes, scooped
1 lemon, juiced
1/2 tsp cayenne pepper
1 C. plain yogurt
1 tsp salt

2 plum tomatoes, seeded and chopped
2 scallions, sliced
1 romaine lettuce hearts
12 flour tortillas

Directions

1. Before you do anything, preheat the grill and grease it.
2. Coat the halibut fillets with some olive oil. Sprinkle over them some salt and pepper.
3. Place the fish fillets on the grill and cook them for 4 to 6 min on each side. Drizzle over them the juice of 1 lime while they're cooking.
4. Get a food processor: Blend in it the avocado flesh, lemon juice, cayenne pepper, yogurt and salt.
5. Pour the mixture into a bowl. Fold into it the diced tomato and scallions to make the guacamole.
6. Heat the tortillas in a pan. Flake the fish and place divide it between the tortillas.
7. Top them with the guacamole followed by the shredded lettuce and your other favorite toppings.
8. Fold your tacos then serve them right away.
9. Enjoy.

SPICY TACO Meatballs with Honey Sauce

Prep Time: 10 mins
Total Time: 35 mins

Servings per Recipe: 4
Calories 569.9
Fat 39.9g
Cholesterol 131.0mg
Sodium 925.0mg
Carbohydrates 17.8g
Protein 34.5g

Ingredients
1 lb ground round
2 tbsp taco seasoning mix
1 (4 oz.) cans mild green chilies, chopped
1 (8 oz.) packages colby-monterey jack cheese, cubed
1 egg white
1 tbsp water
2 C. nacho cheese flavored tortilla chips, crushed
6 tbsp taco sauce, thick style
3 tbsp honey

Directions
1. Before you do anything, preheat the oven to 400 F. Grease a baking sheet.
2. Get a mixing bowl: Mix in it the beef, taco seasoning and green chilies. Shape the mixture into 16 balls.
3. Flatten them slightly and place a cheese side in middle of each ball then pull the meat over it to cover it.
4. Get a mixing bowl: Whisk in it the water with egg white.
5. Coat the meatballs with the egg mixture then roll them in the chips. Press them a little bit then roll them once again the crushed chips.
6. Place the beef meatballs on the greased baking sheet. Grease them with a cooking spray.
7. Place the pan in the oven and cook them for 16 to 22 min.
8. Get a small mixing bowl: Mix in it the honey with taco sauce. Place it in the microwave and let it cook for 35 sec on high.
9. Place the beef taco meatballs on a serving plate then drizzle over the honey sauce.
10. Enjoy.

Acapulco Tacos

Prep Time: 15 mins
Total Time: 25 mins

Servings per Recipe: 6
Calories   298.1
Fat   15.2g
Cholesterol   44.9mg
Sodium   491.7mg
Carbohydrates   26.0g
Protein   15.5g

Ingredients

- 1 onion, chopped
- 3 tbsp oil
- 8 oz. tomato sauce
- 2 pickled jalapeno peppers, chopped
- 1/4 tsp salt
- 2 C. cooked chicken, chopped
- 12 corn tortillas
- 2 C. guacamole
- 1/2 C. sour cream

Directions

1. Place a large pan over medium heat. Heat 1 tbsp of oil in it. Add the onion and cook it for 3 min.
2. Mix in the tomato sauce, peppers, and salt. Put on the lid and let them cook for 6 min.
3. Fold the chicken into the mixture. Cook them for 3 min. turn off the heat.
4. Place a small pan over medium heat. Heat in it 2 tbsp of oil. Place a tortilla in the hot pan for 12 sec on one side then drain it and place it aside.
5. Repeat the process with the remaining tortillas.
6. Divide the chicken mixture between the tortillas then top them with the guacamole, sour cream, and your other favorite toppings.
7. Fold the tortillas over the filling then serve your tacos right away.
8. Enjoy.

NUTTY
Tacos

Prep Time: 5 mins
Total Time: 5 mins

Servings per Recipe: 2
Calories	400.3
Fat	38.5g
Cholesterol	0.0mg
Sodium	507.3mg
Carbohydrates	10.7g
Protein	10.4g

Ingredients
1 C. raw walnuts
1 tbsp soy sauce
1 tsp garlic powder
1 tsp cumin
1 tsp paprika

Directions
1. Get a blender: Place in it all the ingredients. Process them until they become smooth.
2. Spoon the mixture into tortillas.
3. Serve your tacos right away with your favorite toppings.
4. Enjoy.

Crunchy Burrito Style Tacos

Prep Time: 10 mins
Total Time: 25 mins

Servings per Recipe: 6
Calories   446.3
Fat   16.7g
Cholesterol   53.2mg
Sodium   1008.0mg
Carbohydrates   51.0g
Protein   23.4g

Ingredients

- 6 burrito-size flour tortillas
- 6 corn tortillas
- 1/4 C. cheddar cheese, shredded
- 1 lb ground turkey
- 1 1/4 oz. taco seasoning
- 2 tbsp olive oil
- 1 C. lettuce, shredded
- 1 tomatoes, diced
- sour cream

Directions

1. Place a large pan over medium heat. Heat in it the olive oil. Add the beef and cook it for 9 min.
2. Mix in it the taco seasoning by following the instructions on the package.
3. Preheat the oven broiler. Place in it the tortillas and heat them for few minutes.
4. Before you do anything else, preheat the grill and grease it.
5. Place the seasoned beef mixture in the tortillas then top them with lettuce, tomato and cheese. Roll the tortillas over the filling.
6. Place the tacos over the grill and cook them for 2 to 3 min on each side. Serve them warm.
7. Enjoy.

TIJUANA Tacos

Prep Time: 15 mins
Total Time: 25 mins

Servings per Recipe: 4
Calories   278.4
Fat   8.1g
Cholesterol   37.7mg
Sodium   228.8mg
Carbohydrates   31.9g
Protein   21.8g

Ingredients
2 boneless skinless chicken breasts, cooked
1 cans black beans, undrained
1 C. corn
1/2 C. black olives, chopped
1 jalapeno pepper, chopped
1/2 C. chopped onion
1 tsp minced garlic
1-2 tbsp olive oil
1-2 tbsp chili powder
1/4-1/2 tsp red pepper flakes
1/2 tsp oregano

1-2 tsp cumin
1/2 C. water
salt
4-8 oz. tomato sauce
flour tortilla
sour cream
salsa
shredded cheese
guacamole

Directions
1. Place a large pan over medium heat. Heat in it the olive oil.
2. Sauté in it the onion for 3 min. add the garlic with jalapeno and cook them for 1 min.
3. Stir in the chicken with spices, beans, corn, olives and tomato sauce. Cook them for 8 to 12 min to make the filling.
4. Spoon the filling into tortillas then roll them over the filling.
5. Serve your taco right away with your favorite toppings.
6. Enjoy.

Taco Tenders

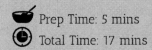
Prep Time: 5 mins
Total Time: 17 mins

Servings per Recipe: 2
Calories   313.4
Fat   4.7g
Cholesterol   143.7mg
Sodium   646.4mg
Carbohydrates   9.1g
Protein   55.5g

Ingredients
4 boneless skinless chicken breasts
1/2 C. fat-free mayonnaise
3 tbsp skim milk
1 tbsp taco seasoning
Dorito tortilla chips, crushed

Directions
1. Before you do anything, preheat the oven to 400 F. Grease a baking pan.
2. Slice the chicken into stripes.
3. Get a large mixing bowl: Toss in it the chicken stripes with mayonnaise, milk, a pinch of salt and pepper.
4. Place the crushed chips in a shallow bowl. Roll in it the chicken stripes.
5. Place them on the greased pan. Cook them in the oven for 11 to 13 min or until they become golden brown.
6. Serve chicken tacos with your favorite toppings.
7. Enjoy.

BELL TILAPIA Tacos with Peach Salsa

Prep Time: 15 mins
Total Time: 30 mins

Servings per Recipe: 8
Calories   214.8
Fat   9.7g
Cholesterol   36.0mg
Sodium   233.9mg
Carbohydrates   18.7g
Protein   14.7g

Ingredients
1 1/2 C. canned peaches, drained
1 red bell pepper, minced
1/4 C. green onion, thinly sliced
1 tbsp jalapeno pepper
1 tbsp olive oil
1 tbsp lime juice
1 tbsp vinegar
1/4 tsp salt
1/4 tsp pepper
1 lb tilapia fillet
1/4 tsp ground cumin

1/8 tsp garlic powder
1/8 tsp onion powder
1 1/2 C. shredded cabbage
1 tbsp cilantro, chopped
3 tbsp mayonnaise
1 tsp lime juice
1/2 C. Monterey jack cheese
8 taco shells

Directions
1. Before you do anything, preheat the oven to 450 F. Grease a baking sheet with some oil.
2. Get a mixing bowl: Stir in it all the salsa ingredients. Place it in the fridge for 20 min.
3. Get a large mixing bowl: Toss in it the cabbage, cilantro, mayonnaise, and lime juice to make the coleslaw.
4. Season the fish fillets with some salt and pepper. Place them over the baking sheet.
5. Get a small mixing bowl: Mix in it the cumin, garlic and onion powder. Sprinkle it over the fish fillets.
6. Place the fish fillets in the oven and bake them for 10 to 12 min.
7. Sprinkle some cheese in the taco shells then top them with the fish fillets, peach salsa and coleslaw.
8. Serve your tacos with some extra toppings of your choice.
9. Enjoy.

Cheddar Tacos with Lime Dressing

Prep Time: 15 mins
Total Time: 15 mins

Servings per Recipe: 4
Calories 474.1
Fat 18.8g
Cholesterol 47.0mg
Sodium 403.2mg
Carbohydrates 48.3g
Protein 30.6g

Ingredients
1/4 C. chopped seeded tomatoes
1/4 C. chopped fresh cilantro
2 tbsp olive oil
1 tbsp cider vinegar
1 tsp grated lime rind
1 tbsp lime juice
1/4 tsp salt
1/4 tsp ground cumin
1/4 tsp chili powder
1/4 tsp black pepper
1 garlic clove, peeled
8 C. sliced iceberg lettuce

1 1/2 C. chopped cooked chicken breasts
1 C. chopped tomato
1 C. chopped green pepper
1 C. diced red onion
1/2 C. shredded cheddar cheese
1 cans black beans, rinsed and drained
4 C. tortilla chips

Directions
1. Get a blender: Place in it all the dressing ingredients. Blend them smooth. Place it in the fridge until ready to serve.
2. Get a mixing bowl: Toss in it the lettuce with beans, tomato, chicken, pepper, onion, black beans, a pinch of salt and pepper.
3. Add the lime dressing and toss them to coat. Spoon the chicken mixture into taco shells.
4. Serve your taco right away.
5. Enjoy.

AMANDA'S
Carne Asada and Homemade Salsa

Prep Time: 45 mins
Total Time: 45 mins

Servings per Recipe: 6
Calories   379.8
Fat   14.1g
Cholesterol   102.8mg
Sodium   112.6mg
Carbohydrates   27.5g
Protein   35.9g

Ingredients
- 2 lbs flank steaks
- 1/3 C. freshly squeezed lime juice
- 2 tsp garlic powder
- 2 tbsp red pepper flakes
- ground black pepper, to taste
- 2 tbsp oregano
- 4 plum tomatoes, chopped
- 1 jalapeno pepper, chopped
- 1 clove garlic, minced
- 2 green onions, chopped
- 6-8 sprigs cilantro, chopped
- 2 tbsp fresh lime juice
- salt
- 1/3 C. fresh cilantro, chopped
- 1 C. lettuce, shredded
- 1 onion, sliced and grilled
- 4-6 green onions, chopped
- fresh lime wedge
- 12 corn tortillas, warmed

Directions
1. Get a large roasting pan: Whisk in it the garlic powder with lime juice, pepper flakes, oregano, salt and pepper to make the marinade.
2. Place the steaks in the marinade and coat them with it. Cover the pan with a plastic wrap. Place it in the fridge for at least 1 h to marinate.
3. Before you do anything, preheat the grill and grease it.
4. Drain the steaks from the marinade and grill them for 2 to 4 min on each side.
5. Get a mixing bowl: Toss in it all the salsa ingredients.
6. Slice the steaks into stripes. Place them in taco shells then top them with tomato Salsa.
7. Top it with lettuce, cilantro, onion, green onion, and some lime wedges on the side. Serve your tacos instantly.
8. Enjoy.

Ventura Tacos

Prep Time: 10 mins
Total Time: 20 mins

Servings per Recipe: 5
Calories   179.9
Fat   10.3g
Cholesterol   62.6mg
Sodium   565.6mg
Carbohydrates   3.8g
Protein   19.2g

Ingredients

- 1 lb ground turkey
- 1 bunch lettuce
- 1-2 garlic clove, chopped
- 1 tbsp canola oil
- 1 tbsp chili powder
- 1/4 tsp garlic powder
- 1/4 tsp onion powder
- 1/4 tsp red pepper flakes
- 1/4 tsp dried oregano
- 1/2 tsp paprika
- 1 1/2 tsp cumin
- 1 tsp salt
- 1 tsp pepper
- chopped onion
- chopped cilantro
- shredded cheddar cheese
- light sour cream

Directions

1. Place a large pan over medium heat. Heat in it the oil. Add the turkey and cook it for 5 min.
2. Get a small mixing bowl: Combine in it the taco seasoning ingredients. Mix them into the cooked turkey with garlic.
3. Spoon the mixture into taco shells. Top them with some lettuce, onion, cilantro, cheese and sour cream.
4. Serve your tacos right away.
5. Enjoy.

PORTUGUESE
Breakfast Tacos

Prep Time: 10 mins
Total Time: 30 mins

Servings per Recipe: 2
Calories   975.9
Fat   70.8g
Cholesterol   528.7mg
Sodium   1806.7mg
Carbohydrates   27.1g
Protein   56.2g

Ingredients

4 corn tortillas
1 C. grated white cheddar cheese
4 large eggs
4 tbsp chopped fresh cilantro, divided

7 oz. beef sausage, or Italian turkey sausage
4 green onions, sliced
sour cream
hot sauce

Directions

1. Place a large pan over medium heat. Grease it with some oil. Heat in it the tortillas for 1 to 2 min on each side.
2. Sprinkle 1/4 C. of cheese over each tortilla. Place it aside.
3. Get a small mixing bowl: Mix in it the eggs with 2 tbsp of cilantro, a pinch of salt and pepper.
4. Place a large pan over medium heat. Cook in it the sausage for 6 min. Mix in it the green onions and cook them for an extra 3 min.
5. Stir in the eggs mix and cook them for 1 to 2 min while stirring them all the time.
6. Place the tortillas pan over medium heat. Cook them for 1 to 2 min until they become slightly crispy on the side.
7. Place cheesy tortilla in medium pan. Cook it for 1 to 2 min to heat it through. Turn off the heat.
8. Spoon 1/4 of the sausage mixture over the cheese layer, top it with some cilantro then fold the tortilla over the filling.
9. Repeat the process with the remaining tortillas. Serve you tacos right away with some sour cream and cheese
10. Enjoy.

Cast Iron Tacos

Prep Time: 10 mins
Total Time: 30 mins

Servings per Recipe: 8
Calories   412.5
Fat   19.8g
Cholesterol   83.1mg
Sodium   652.1mg
Carbohydrates   36.1g
Protein   22.7g

Ingredients
- 1 lb ground beef
- 1/2 onion, chopped
- 1 envelope taco seasoning mix
- 1 cans kidney beans, drained well
- 1 C. kernel corn
- 1 boxes corn muffin mix
- 1/3 C. low-fat milk
- 1 egg
- 1/2 C. cheddar cheese, shredded
- 2 tbsp chopped jalapenos
- 1 C. Monterey jack cheese
- 1 C. shredded lettuce
- 1/4 C. chopped tomato
- 1 dollop sour cream
- 1 dollop guacamole

Directions
1. Before you do anything, preheat the oven to 450 F. Grease a baking pan.
2. Place a large pan over medium heat. Cook in it the beef for 9 min. discard the grease.
3. Mix thee beans with corn, a pinch of salt and pepper into the cooked beef. Cook them for an extra 3 min.
4. Get a mixing bowl: Whisk in it the corn muffin mix with milk and eggs. Fold the jalapenos and cheddar into the batter.
5. Pour the muffin corn mixture in the greased pan. Spread over it the beef mixture leaving the sides empty.
6. Place the taco pan in the oven and cook it for 16 min. Top it with jack cheese then bake it for an extra 3 min.
7. Garnish your cornbread taco with lettuce, tomato, sour cream and guacamole. Serve warm.
8. Enjoy.

HOT CRISPY
Taco Wings

Prep Time: 15 mins
Total Time: 1 hr 5 mins

Servings per Recipe: 4
Calories   522.2
Fat   36.5g
Cholesterol   174.7mg
Sodium   170.7mg
Carbohydrates   3.8g
Protein   41.9g

Ingredients
1 envelopes taco seasoning mix
1 tbsp cornstarch
1 tbsp cornmeal
1/2-1 tsp chili powder
1 tsp ground cumin
1 tsp dried oregano
2 lbs chicken wings

Directions
1. Before you do anything, preheat the oven to 350 F. Line up a baking sheet with a parchment paper.
2. Get a large zip lock bag: Combine in it the taco seasoning with cornstarch, chili, cornmeal, oregano, cumin, a pinch of salt and pepper.
3. Place in it the chicken wings then seal the bag and shake it to coat them.
4. Place the pan in the oven and cook it for 25 min. Flip the chicken wings and cook them for an extra 25 min.
5. Serve your taco chicken wings with your favorite dip.
6. Enjoy.

California Cream Tacos

Prep Time: 30 mins
Total Time: 30 mins

Servings per Recipe: 4
Calories 693.8
Fat 49.1g
Cholesterol 75.0mg
Sodium 886.0mg
Carbohydrates 54.3g
Protein 14.4g

Ingredients

1 packages cream cheese, softened
1/2 C. sour cream
1 cans chopped green chilies, drained
1 tbsp taco seasoning
4 flour tortillas, warmed
2 medium ripe avocados, peeled and sliced
2 plum tomatoes, thinly sliced
5 green onions, sliced
1 cans sliced ripe olives, drained

Directions

1. Get a mixing bowl: Mix in it the cream cheese, sour cream, chilies and taco seasoning.
2. Place a tortilla on a serving plate. Spread in it 1/2 C. of the cream mixture. Top it with avocados, tomatoes, onions and olives.
3. Fold the tortilla over the filling. Repeat the process with the remaining tortillas. Serve them right away.
4. Enjoy.

MEXICAN
Cheesy Bread

Prep Time: 10 mins
Total Time: 3 hr 50 mins

Servings per Recipe: 1
Calories 1893.6
Fat 41.5g
Cholesterol 118.6mg
Sodium 2678.3mg
Carbohydrates 304.1g
Protein 69.3g

Ingredients

1 C. water, plus
2 tbsp water
3 C. bread flour
1 C. shredded cheddar cheese
1 tbsp taco seasoning mix
1 tbsp granulated sugar
3/4 tsp salt
1 1/2 tsp yeast

Directions

1. Combine all the ingredients in your bread machine.
2. Press the basic/white cycle. Select the light to medium crust color.
3. Allow the taco breads to cool down completely. Serve them right away.
4. Enjoy.

Taco Fiesta Pan

🥣 Prep Time: 15 mins
🕐 Total Time: 40 mins

Servings per Recipe: 4
Calories   564.5
Fat   26.9g
Cholesterol   106.7mg
Sodium   264.8mg
Carbohydrates   45.7g
Protein   33.0g

Ingredients
- 1 lb ground beef
- 1 large onion, diced
- 1 cans diced tomatoes
- 1 C. uncooked long grain rice
- 1 package taco seasoning
- 1 C. shredded cheddar cheese
- 2 C. shredded lettuce

Directions
1. Place a large pan over medium heat. Brown in it the beef with onion for 8 min. discard the grease.
2. Reserve the tomato juice. Stir the drained tomato into the beef pan with 1 to 1 1/2 C. of water, rice, and taco seasoning.
3. Cook them until they start boiling. Put on the lid and lower the heat. Let them cook for 26 min.
4. Top your taco pan with some cheese and lettuce. Serve it hot.
5. Enjoy.

ELIZABETH'S Taco Family Casserole

Prep Time: 15 mins
Total Time: 50 mins

Servings per Recipe: 8
Calories	691.6
Fat	37.5g
Cholesterol	167.4mg
Sodium	1253.9mg
Carbohydrates	51.9g
Protein	36.9g

Ingredients

- 1 lb ground beef
- 1 lb ground turkey, optional
- 2 packages taco seasoning mix
- 1/2 C. diced green pepper
- 1 cans tomato sauce
- 1 cans diced tomatoes
- 1 lb bow tie pasta
- 2 C. shredded Monterey jack cheese
- 1 C. sour cream

Directions

1. Before you do anything, preheat the oven to 350 F. Grease a baking pan.
2. Place a large pan over medium heat. Cook in it the turkey with beef for 12 min.
3. Mix in the taco seasoning mix, tomato sauce, diced tomatoes and green pepper. Cook them until they start boiling.
4. Lower the heat and let them cook for 12 min.
5. Prepare the pasta by following the instructions on the package. Remove it from the water.
6. Get a large mixing bowl: Toss in it the pasta with 1 C. of sour cream and cheese.
7. Place the creamy pasta into the greased pan. Spread over it the saucy beef mixture.
8. Place the taco pan in the oven and let it cook for 38 to 42 min. Serve it hot.
9. Enjoy.

Mexicorn Tacos

Prep Time: 20 mins
Total Time: 20 mins

Servings per Recipe: 6
Calories   354.1
Fat   10.2g
Cholesterol   65.2mg
Sodium   492.3mg
Carbohydrates   40.4g
Protein   27.2g

Ingredients

- 1 1/4 lbs lean ground turkey
- 1 1/4 oz. taco seasoning mix
- 1 cans black beans, rinsed and drained
- 1 cans mexicorn, undrained, or corn
- 1/4 C. water
- 6 flour tortillas

Directions

1. Place a large pan over medium heat. Brown in it the turkey for 8 min.
2. Mix in the taco seasoning with black beans, mexicorn, water, a pinch of salt and pepper.
3. Let them cook for another 8 min while stirring them often. Spoon the mixture into taco shells then serve it with your favorite toppings.
4. Enjoy.

CHICAGO
Deep Dish Taco

Prep Time: 20 mins
Total Time: 45 mins

Servings per Recipe: 8
Calories 386.8
Fat 24.1g
Cholesterol 69.5mg
Sodium 623.8mg
Carbohydrates 24.3g
Protein 17.8g

Ingredients
2 C. biscuit mix
1/2 C. cold water
1 lb ground beef
1 green pepper, chopped
1 small onion, chopped
1 cans tomato sauce

1 cartons sour cream
1 C. cheddar cheese, shredded
1/3 C. mayonnaise
paprika

Directions
1. Before you do anything, preheat the oven to 350 F. Grease a baking pan.
2. Get a mixing bowl: Stir in it the water with biscuit mix well. Press the mixture into the greased pan.
3. Place it in the oven and let it cook for 10 min to make the crust
4. Place a large pan over medium heat. Brown in it the beef, green pepper, onion, a pinch of salt and pepper for 3 min.
5. Mix in the tomato sauce. Spread the mixture over the crust.
6. Get a mixing bowl: Stir in it the sour cream, cheese, and mayonnaise. Spread it over sauce layer.
7. Adjust the oven heat to 375 F.
8. Top it with a dash of paprika. Place the pan in the oven and let it cook for 26 min.
9. Slice the taco pie into squares then serve them warm with your favorite toppings.
10. Enjoy.

Japanese Beef Sausage Tacos

🥣 Prep Time: 20 mins
⏱ Total Time: 45 mins

Servings per Recipe: 4
Calories   644.5
Fat   34.9g
Cholesterol   74.9mg
Sodium   1093.8mg
Carbohydrates   56.3g
Protein   27.5g

Ingredients

12 oz. beef sausage, casings removed, or italian turkey sausage
1 medium white onion, sliced
6 oz. shiitake mushrooms, sliced
12 oz. Yukon gold potatoes, grated
salt

1/2 C. chopped fresh cilantro
12 corn tortillas, warmed
roasted tomatillo salsa

Directions

1. Place a large pan over medium heat. Cook in it the sausage for 6 min.
2. Stir in the onion with mushroom. Cook them for 4 min.
3. Add the grated potato and mix them well. Let them cook for 12 to 16 min or until it is done.
4. Spoon the mixture into taco shells and garnish them with some cilantro.
5. Serve your tacos right away with some tomatillo salsa and your favorite toppings.
6. Enjoy.

BLACK TACOS
with Brown Rice

Prep Time: 20 mins
Total Time: 40 mins

Servings per Recipe: 15
Calories   161.9
Fat   1.5g
Cholesterol   0.0mg
Sodium   25.1mg
Carbohydrates   31.9g
Protein   6.3g

Ingredients
2 C. cooked brown rice
2 cans black beans, undrained
1 C. picante salsa
1 C. chopped onion
3-4 chopped garlic cloves
3-4 fresh jalapeno peppers, chopped
1 tbsp chili powder
1 tbsp ground cumin
20 corn tortillas

Directions
1. Place a large pan over medium heat. Heat in it 3 tbsp of vegetable oil.
2. Sauté in it the onion for 3 min. add the garlic with jalapeno peppers and cook them for 2 min.
3. Stir in the beans with rice, salsa, chili powder, cumin, a pinch of salt and pepper.
4. Cook them until they start boiling. Turn off the heat.
5. Place a large deep pan over medium heat. Heat in it a splash of oil. Cook in it the tortillas until they become crisp on the sides.
6. Spoon the bean mixture into the taco shells. Serve them with your favorite toppings.
7. Enjoy.

Mexican
Tacos Sea Shells

Prep Time: 10 mins
Total Time: 50 mins

Servings per Recipe: 4
Calories 753.7
Fat 57.7g
Cholesterol 200.8mg
Sodium 1490.2mg
Carbohydrates 8.6g
Protein 48.3g

Ingredients
1 1/2 lbs ground beef
1 packages cream cheese with chives, cubed and softened
1 tsp salt
1 tsp chili powder
18 jumbo pasta shells, cooked
2 tsp butter, melted
1 C. prepared taco sauce
1 C. shredded cheddar cheese
1 C. shredded Monterey jack cheese
1 1/2 C. crushed tortilla chips
1 C. sour cream
chopped green onion

Directions
1. Before you do anything, preheat the oven to 350 F. Grease a baking pan.
2. Place a large pan over medium heat. Cook in it the beef for 8 min.
3. Mix in it the cream cheese, salt, and chili powder. Cook them for 6 min over low heat.
4. Get a large mixing bowl: Stir in it the pasta shells with butter.
5. Spoon the beef mixture into the pasta shells then place them in the greased pan.
6. Drizzle the taco sauce all over the stuffed pasta shells. Lay a piece of foil over it to cover it.
7. Cook the pasta pan in the oven for 16 min. Discard the foil and top it with cheese and chips.
8. Cook it for an extra 16 min. Serve your taco casserole hot with your favorite toppings.
9. Enjoy.

HOT TACO
Scoops

Prep Time: 5 mins
Total Time: 10 mins

Servings per Recipe: 48
Calories   15.1
Fat   0.6g
Cholesterol   2.8mg
Sodium   44.1mg
Carbohydrates   1.2g
Protein   1.0g

Ingredients

48 corn tortilla chips, scoop style
3/4 C. sour cream
1 1/2 tsp taco seasoning
1 cans no-bean chili
1/2 C. cheddar cheese, shredded

Directions

1. Before you do anything, preheat the oven broiler.
2. Place 1 tsp of chili in each tortilla C. Top it with 1 tsp of cheese.
3. Place the tortilla C. in a lined up baking pan. Cook them in the oven for 2 min.
4. Drizzle the cream sauce over the taco C. then serve them with your favorite toppings.
5. Enjoy.

Onondaga Territory Tacos

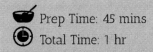

Prep Time: 45 mins
Total Time: 1 hr

Servings per Recipe: 10
Calories   422.9
Fat   12.6g
Cholesterol   52.4mg
Sodium   431.6mg
Carbohydrates   52.6g
Protein   23.2g

Ingredients

4-5 C. flour
3 1/2 tsp baking powder
1 tsp salt
1/2 C. instant milk
2 C. water
1 1/2 lbs ground beef
1 onion, chopped
3/4 tsp garlic salt
1 can pinto beans
grated cheese
salsa
lettuce
tomatoes
onion
sour cream
green onion

Directions

1. To make the dough:
2. Get a mixing bowl: Mix in it the flour with baking powder, salt, milk and water.
3. Shape the dough into a ball. Wrap it in a plastic wrap and let it rest for 16 min.
4. Place a large pan over medium heat. Heat 1 tbsp of oil in it.
5. Roll the dough on floured surface. Use a cookie cutter to cut it into thin 8 inches circles.
6. Cook the dough circles in the hot oil in batches until they become golden brown.
7. To make the filling:
8. Place a large pan over medium heat. Cook in it the beef with onion for 8 min. discard the fat.
9. Mix in the garlic salt with beans. Cook them for 12 to 16 min over low heat.
10. Place the crispy fried circles on a serving plates. Top them with the beef mixture.
11. Serve your taco bites right away with your favorite toppings.
12. Enjoy.

SOUTHWEST
Quiches

Prep Time: 20 mins
Total Time: 50 mins

Servings per Recipe: 12
Calories	151.4
Fat	8.2g
Cholesterol	48.3mg
Sodium	556.7mg
Carbohydrates	8.7g
Protein	10.5g

Ingredients
1 lb lean ground beef
1/3 C. chopped onion
1/3 C. sliced black olives
1 cans tomato sauce
1/4 C. water
1 packages taco seasoning mix
2 tbsp hot sauce

1 egg, beaten
4 flour tortillas
1/3 C. sour cream
1/2 C. shredded cheddar cheese

Directions
1. Before you do anything, preheat the oven to 350 F. Grease a muffin pan.
2. Place a large pan over medium heat. Brown in it the onion with beef for 8 min. Discard the fat.
3. Mix in the olives, tomato sauce, 1/4 C. water, taco seasoning, hot sauce and egg. Turn off the heat.
4. Use 3 inches cookie cutter circle to cut each tortilla into 3 rounds. Place the tortilla circles in the greased muffin C.
5. Spoon the beef mixture over the tortilla C. Top them with sour cream and cheese. Cook them for 26 min in the oven.
6. Serve your taco muffins with your favorite toppings.
7. Enjoy.

Saucy Taco Noodles Casserole

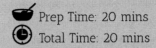 Prep Time: 20 mins
Total Time: 20 mins

Servings per Recipe: 6
Calories   507.2
Fat   16.5g
Cholesterol   77.6mg
Sodium   166.9mg
Carbohydrates   59.0g
Protein   28.6g

Ingredients

- 16 oz. pasta
- 3 C. cubed cooked chicken
- 1 tsp minced garlic
- 3 tsp olive oil
- 1 C. half-and-half cream
- 5-6 tsp taco seasoning
- 2 tbsp butter
- parmesan cheese, to taste

Directions

1. Prepare the pasta by following the instructions on the package.
2. Place a large pan over medium heat. Heat in it the olive oil.
3. Add the chicken with garlic and cook them for 6 min. Mix in the butter with taco seasoning, half-and-half, a pinch of salt and pepper.
4. Cook them for an extra 2 to 3 min. Stir in the pasta.
5. Serve your taco pasta with some grated cheese and toppings of your choice.
6. Enjoy.

SECRET Tacos

Prep Time: 15 mins
Total Time: 18 mins

Servings per Recipe: 4
Calories	289.1
Fat	12.3g
Cholesterol	100.3mg
Sodium	459.9mg
Carbohydrates	5.8g
Protein	37.4g

Ingredients

- 2 tbsp cream cheese
- 2 tbsp sour cream
- 2 tsp minced canned jalapeno slices
- 2 tsp jalapeno juice, from jar
- 3/4 tsp Splenda granular
- 1/2 tsp paprika
- 1/2 tsp cumin
- 1/8 tsp cayenne pepper
- 1/8 tsp garlic powder
- 1 lb boneless skinless chicken breast
- 1 zucchini, sliced long thinly
- 1 onion, sliced
- 4 tortillas
- 1 C. cheddar cheese, shredded
- 1/2 C. Monterey jack cheese, shredded

Directions

1. Before you do anything, preheat the grill and grease it.
2. Get a mixing bowl: Place in it the cream cheese with sour cream, jalapeno slices and juice, Splenda sugar, paprika, cumin, cayenne pepper, garlic powder and a pinch of salt.
3. Mix them well to make the sauce.
4. Sprinkle the chicken breasts with some salt and pepper. Cook them on the grill for 4 to 6 min on each side. Thinly slice it.
5. Place a large pan over medium heat. Place in it a tortilla.
6. Top it half of it with 1/4 C. of shredded cheddar cheese and the other half with 1/4 C. of shredded cheese.
7. Lay on one side of the tortilla 1/4 C. of sliced chicken followed by 1/4 zucchini, and onion.
8. Drizzle 1 tbsp of over the cheesy side. Pull it over the veggies and chicken side then press it with a spatula.
9. Press it gently and let it cook for 1 min. Repeat the process with the remaining ingredients.
10. Serve your tacos right away with your favorite toppings.
11. Enjoy.

Spanish Style Taco Pan

Prep Time: 10 mins
Total Time: 40 mins

Servings per Recipe: 6
Calories   566.8
Fat   24.3g
Cholesterol   90.9mg
Sodium   293.0mg
Carbohydrates   56.3g
Protein   28.6g

Ingredients
1 lb ground beef
1 C. onion, diced
1 package taco seasoning mix
1 (16 oz.) cans tomatoes, diced
2 C. white rice
2 C. cheddar cheese, shredded

Directions
1. Place a large saucepan over medium heat. Cook in it the beef for 9 min. discard the fat.
2. Mix in it the onion, taco seasoning packet, cooked rice and tomatoes. Let them cook for 32 min over low heat.
3. Spoon the mixture into taco shells. Garnish them with some lettuce, taco chips, tomatoes, sour cream and cheese.
4. Serve your tacos right away.
5. Enjoy.

HALIBUT
BBQ Tacos

Prep Time: 15 mins
Total Time: 25 mins

Servings per Recipe: 4
Calories 428.4
Fat 10.3g
Cholesterol 109.6mg
Sodium 838.7mg
Carbohydrates 36.3g
Protein 44.7g

Ingredients
1 1/2 lbs halibut fillets, chunks
2-3 tbsp cajun seasoning
2 C. shredded green cabbage
1 C. shredded red cabbage
1/4 C. cider vinegar
1/4 C. sour cream
6 green onions, chopped
1/2-1 tsp salt

8 flour tortillas
lemon wedge
salsa
tartar sauce
guacamole

Directions
1. Before you do anything, preheat the grill.
2. Get a mixing bowl: Stir in it the halibut fish with Cajun seasoning.
3. Get a grilling wok and grease it with some oil. Place in it the halibut fish then cook it over the hot coals for 9 to 12 min.
4. Get a small mixing bowl: Whisk in it the vinegar, sour cream, green onions, and salt. Stir in the cabbage.
5. Add them to the halibut mix and toss them to coat. Divide the mixture between the taco shells then top them with the halibut chunks.
6. Serve your tacos with your favorite toppings.
7. Enjoy.

Gyros Style Tacos with Yogurt Sauce

Prep Time: 15 mins
Total Time: 25 mins

Servings per Recipe: 2
Calories 525.5
Fat 25.7g
Cholesterol 116.0mg
Sodium 887.8mg
Carbohydrates 33.3g
Protein 39.0g

Ingredients

1/2 C. Greek yogurt
1 gherkin, finely diced
2 tbsp black olives, pitted and sliced
2 garlic cloves
1/2 tsp lemon juice
1 tsp olive oil
1/4 tsp dill, dried
black pepper, to taste

4 large taco shells
250 g cooked chicken, diced
1 large tomatoes, sliced into 8 pieces
1 C. mixed salad greens
2 oz. feta, crumbled

Directions

1. Get a mixing bowl: Mix in it the sauce ingredients. Stir in the chicken. Place it in the fridge until ready to serve.
2. Heat the taco shells by following the instructions on the package.
3. Lay 2 tomato slices on a taco shell then top it with some lettuce, and the saucy chicken mixture.
4. Repeat the process with the remaining tacos.
5. Garnish your tacos with some feta cheese then serve them.
6. Enjoy.

SEASONED
Taco Chips

Prep Time: 10 mins
Total Time: 23 mins

Servings per Recipe: 4
Calories   212.9
Fat   15.8g
Cholesterol   0.0mg
Sodium   1935.1mg
Carbohydrates   15.4g
Protein   2.4g

Ingredients
4 flour tortillas
4 tbsp olive oil
1 tbsp salt
1 tbsp pepper

Directions
1. Before you do anything, preheat the oven to 350 F. Grease a baking pan.
2. Coat the tortillas lightly with some oil. Season them with some salt and pepper.
3. Place a tortilla in an ovenproof bowl. Cook it in the oven for 14 min. Place it aside until it cools down completely.
4. Repeat the process with the remaining tortillas.
5. Serve your taco bowls with your favorite filling and toppings.
6. Enjoy.

Creamy Taco Stroganoff Casserole

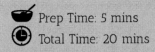

Prep Time: 5 mins
Total Time: 20 mins

Servings per Recipe: 4
Calories   876.4
Fat   49.9g
Cholesterol   217.1mg
Sodium   447.1mg
Carbohydrates   66.4g
Protein   43.2g

Ingredients

- 1 small onion, chopped
- 1 lb ground beef
- 1 envelopes taco seasoning mix
- 1/2 C. water
- 1 cans corn, drained
- 1 packages cream cheese
- 1 C. shredded cheddar cheese
- 8 oz. egg noodles, cooked

Directions

1. Place a large pan over medium heat. Brown in it the beef with onion for 8 min. discard the grease.
2. Mix in it the taco seasoning with water and corn. Cook them for 2 min.
3. Stir in the cheddar cheese with cream cheese. Cook them for 3 min while stirring them often.
4. Spoon the taco sauce over the cooked noodles. Serve them with your favorite toppings.
5. Enjoy.

LATIN
Garlic Steak Tacos

Prep Time: 5 mins
Total Time: 25 mins

Servings per Recipe: 4
Calories	498.5
Fat	32.3g
Cholesterol	92.9mg
Sodium	123.5mg
Carbohydrates	1.6g
Protein	48.2g

Ingredients
2 lbs flank steaks
2 medium limes, juice
1/4 C. fresh cilantro, chopped
1 pinch garlic pepper seasoning
1/4 C. extra virgin olive oil

Directions
1. Before you do anything, preheat the grill and grease it.
2. Get a mixing bowl: Mix in it the juice of the two limes, a small bunch of cilantro, garlic pepper, and a splash of olive oil to make the marinade.
3. Season the steaks with some salt and pepper. Coat them with the marinade. Cover the bowl and place it in the fridge for at least 60 min.
4. Once the time is up, drain the steaks and cook them on the grill for 9 to 12 min on each side. Thinly slice them.
5. Place the steak slices in taco shells. Top them with your favorite toppings.
6. Enjoy.